DEATH AND THE AFTERLIFE

DEATH AND THE AFTERLIFE

EDITED BY JACOB NEUSNER

WIPF & STOCK · Eugene, Oregon

Wipf and Stock Publishers
199 W 8th Ave, Suite 3
Eugene, OR 97401

Death and the Afterlife
By Neusner, Jacob
Copyright©2000 Pilgrim Press
ISBN 13: 978-1-60899-414-4
Publication date 2/17/2010
Previously published by Pilgrim Press, 2000

CONTENTS

Preface   *vii*

Contributors   *xi*

Introduction · JACOB NEUSNER   *xiii*

1   Buddhism · CHARLES HALLISEY   *1*

2   Judaism · JACOB NEUSNER   *30*

3   Islam · JONATHAN E. BROCKOPP   *60*

4   Christianity · BRUCE CHILTON   *79*

5   Hinduism · BRIAN K. SMITH   *97*

Literary Sources of the World Religions   *117*

Notes   *135*

The great world religions address certain existential issues in common, for the human situation raises compelling questions that transcend the limits of time, space, and circumstance. Recognizing that each religion forms a system with its own definitive traits, we aver that all religions must and do treat in common a range of fundamental topics. We hold that comparison and contrast among religions begin in the treatment of urgent questions that all of them must address and somehow resolve. This library introduces the religions of the world as they meet in conversation on the profound issues of world order— transcendent, individual and familial, and social. In the first rubric falls how we know God; in the second, our life of suffering and death, women and families, and the aspiration for afterlife; and in the third, the authority and continuity of tradition itself. Indeed, for the purpose of these volumes we may define religion as a theory of the social order that addresses from the unique perspective of transcendence (some prefer "the sacred," others, "God," in concrete language) issues of the human condition of home and family, on the one side, and of the public interest, on the other.

The five topics of the initial account require only brief clarification. Common to the human condition is the quest for God. Every religion identifies authoritative teaching ("sacred texts"), though what the various religions mean by "a text" will vary, since a person or a drama or a dance as much as a piece of writing may form a fixed and official statement for amplification and exegesis through time. In these five volumes, the initial set in the Pilgrim Library of World Religions, we take up the five topics we deem both critical and ubiquitous in the religions we identify as paramount. Following a single outline, worked out in common, we spell out how each religion addresses the topic at hand. In this way we propose to make possible a labor of comparison of religions: how all address a single issue, uniformly defined.

The religions are chosen because all of them not only speak to humanity in common but also relate to one another in concrete, historical ways. Judaism, Christianity, and Islam join together in a common doctrine of the unity of God and in valuing a common scripture—the Hebrew Scriptures of ancient Israel. Judaism knows these Scriptures as the written Torah, which is the Old Testament of Christianity. In the case of Christianity and Islam, the Old and New Testaments are joined into the Bible, "the Book." Hinduism forms the matrix out of which Buddhism took shape, much as ancient Israelite Scriptures, amplified by the Judaism of the day, defined the matrix in which Christianity originated. Not only do Judaism, Christianity, and Islam conduct an ongoing dialogue between and among themselves, but Christianity and Islam compete in Africa, and Hinduism and Islam in India. Buddhism in the twentieth century has become a global religion, found on every continent. All five religions not only address humanity but reach across the boundaries of ethnic groups and local societies and speak of the condition of humanity. And all five come to formulation in a set of writings deemed classical and authoritative.

That fact—that each of the religions treated here identifies a canon that defines the faith—makes the work possible. For each of the religions treated here proves diverse; viewed over time, all of them yield marks of historical change and diversity of doctrine and practice alike. Take Judaism, for example. Today it comprises a number of distinct religious systems, or Judaisms—for example, Reform, Orthodox, and Conservative in North America. Christianity has three vast divisions: Catholic, Protestant, and Orthodox. The world has gotten to know some of the differences between Shiite and Sunni Islam. The prominence of the Dalai Lama, as the leader of the Tibetan Buddhist community, has made us aware of the cultural diversity of Buddhism. Hinduism is a diverse conglomeration of sects and traditions, sometimes organized into three general categories: Vaishnavas (worshipers of Vichnu), Shaivites (who regard Shiva as the principal deity), and Shaktas (who see the Goddess as supreme). The upshot is that while we recognize the density and diversity of each of the religions under study in these volumes, our account of their principal doctrines on critical and universal issues appeals only to those writings that all forms or versions of the several religions acknowledge, to which all Judaisms or Christianities, for instance, will appeal.

That same fact—the appeal to authoritative writings of a classical character—also permits us to describe without nuance of context or historical circumstance the positions of the five religions. People who practice the religions set forth here may believe diverse things within the respective framework of those religions; Catholics may practice birth control, for example. So, too, religions that bear a distinctive relationship to a given ethnic group—Judaism to Jews, for instance—cannot be defined merely by public-opinion polling of that ethnic group. Not all Jews practice Judaism, not all Arabs, Islam; and not all Italians, Catholicism. By concentrating on the classical statements of the religions at hand, we set forth an ideal type, the picture of the religion that its authoritative writings provide, not the picture of the religion that the workaday world may yield.

The same consideration affects the diversity over time and in contemporary life of the several religions before us. Everyone understands that all five religions not only produced diverse systems, but also developed and changed over history, so that a doctrine or belief on a given topic in one time and place may not conform to the shape of the same doctrine or belief on the same topic in a different setting. Ideas about God vary, for instance, depending on the situation of the interpreter—learned or mystic or simple, for instance—or on the age in which the idea is explained. That is quite natural, given the vast stretches of time and space traversed by the five religions we examine. While acknowledging the variations produced by the passage of time and the movement of culture, we appeal to the classical writings for an account that all later generations of the faithful, wherever located, can affirm, however diverse the interpretations placed upon that account. In the appendix, Literary Sources of the World Religions, each of the writers lists the documents that form the foundation of his chapter in this volume.

This library took shape in the shared intellectual adventure that joins some of us together as professors of the academic study of religion at Bard College and in dialogue with our students there. We tried out the various chapters on them.

All of us express our appreciation to the president of Bard College, Dr. Leon Botstein, and dean of faculty Stuart Levine for their encouragement of this project; and to Richard Brown, formerly of Pilgrim Press, our patient and gentle editor, whose good ideas always made the work still more challenging and stimulating than our joint venture had made it to begin with.

CONTRIBUTORS

JONATHAN E. BROCKOPP received his Ph.D. from Yale University. He is assistant professor of religion at Bard College.

BRUCE CHILTON is chairman of the Department of Religion, Bernard Iddings Bell Professor of Religion, and chaplain at Bard College.

CHARLES HALLISEY is John L. Loeb Associate Professor of the Humanities at Harvard University.

JACOB NEUSNER is distinguished research professor of religious studies at the University of South Florida and research professor of theology and religion at Bard College.

BRIAN K. SMITH is professor of religious studies at the University of California, Riverside.

INTRODUCTION

Those who would like to view religion in a generic way, speaking of how all religions concur on a few matters, find in the experience of death a point in common. Everyone is born and dies, and every religion sets forth both doctrine and deed in response to that universal experience. The earliest material evidence of religious aspiration and expression occurs in the setting of burials and the archaeology of grave rites. Hence if we wish to compose an account of "religion in general"—just as people would like to write prayers "that all of us can recite," for use in schools, for instance—we ought to have come to the right topic. Surely when we address the theme of the present volume, death and the afterlife, we should find evidence of the generic religion that some seek. All religions concur that death demands discussion.

But in the pages of this book, readers will find ample reason to doubt that much generalization about religion will survive the work of comparison and contrast. No more powerful argument against the conception that, basically, religions say the same thing comes to hand than the actualities of religions' discussions of death and the afterlife. In these pages we learn that each religion tells its own story in its own way. Although the monotheist religions, Judaism, Christianity, and Islam, concur on basic principles, they differ in details as radically as Buddhism and Hinduism differ from the three of them. Just as there is no such thing as a prayer upon which all religions can agree to recite in common, so other components of the alleged, generic religion prove difficult to identify and define. Religions contrast much more than they concur.

That does not mean there is no such thing as "religion," but only "religions." The comparison and contrast of religions yield the possibility of speaking about "religion," not solely "religions." Comparison comes before contrast, establishing grounds based on shared traits prior to distinguishing points of reference. Not only does everyone die, but all religions address death and such issues as afterlife that death raises. We find ourselves on solid ground, therefore, when in the present context we undertake the comparison and contrast of such world religions of humanity as Islam, Buddhism, Judaism, Hinduism, and Christianity, all viewed as ideal types. Here the shared experience of humanity defines the common ground that sustains the construction of contrasting models. But what do we find when we come to the specific religions treated here?

All religions concur that death forms the occasion for wise reflection, but they draw diverse conclusions. Within each of the great traditions, moreover, characterizing doctrine proves difficult. Buddhists learn from but would escape death. That means, ultimately, not undergoing "birth again and again," which is misery. Old age, sickness, and death come about by reason of birth, and Buddhists would find the way to end the process of being born again and again. Death attests to impermanence, "only another instance of the flux that characterizes all existence." As to the afterlife, "the craving for future existence was the cause of birth and thus the condition for death again in the future." To die well is to die in a serene spirit. To reach the end of death is to attain bliss. "Through our desires and our consequent actions," Charles Hallisey says, "we are reborn again and again in the various conditions of this world, and with each birth, we again get death." To overcome death, one has to attain the real afterlife, something that takes place in this life with the help of death.

For Judaism, by contrast, with its stout affirmation of life, death comes about by reason of sin. But then death atones for sin, leaving a person ready to stand in judgment and gain "a portion in the world to come," or resurrection from the grave at the end of time. Death does not mark the end of the individual human life; exile does not mark the last stop in the journey of Holy Israel. Israelites will live in the age or the world to come, all Israel in the land of Israel, comparable to Eden; and Israel will comprehend all who know the one true God. The restoration of world order that completes the demonstration of God's justice encompasses both private life and the domain of all Israel. For both, restorationist theology provides eternal life; to be Israel means to live. As far as the individual is concerned, beyond the grave, at a determinate moment, the individual (1) rises from the grave in resurrection, (2) is judged, and (3) enjoys the world to come. For the entirety of Israel, congruently, all Israel participates in the resurrection, which takes place in the land of Israel, and enters the world to come. The last things are to be known from the first. In the just plan of creation, humanity was meant to live in Eden, and Israel in the land of Israel in time without end. The restoration will bring about the long and tragically postponed perfection of the world order, sealing the demonstration of the justice of God's plan for creation. Risen from the dead, having atoned through death, human beings will be judged in accord with their deeds. Israel for its part, when it repents and conforms its will to God's, recovers its Eden. The consequences of rebellion and sin having been overcome, the struggle of the human will and God's word having been resolved, God's original plan will be realized at last.

The simple, global logic of the system, with its focus on the world order of justice established by God but disrupted by humanity, leads inexorably to this eschatology of restoration, the restoration of balance, order, proportion yielding eternity. Without judgment and eternal life for the righteous, this world's imbalance cannot be righted, nor can God's justice be revealed. Monotheism without an eschatology of judgment and the world to come leaves unresolved the tensions inherent in the starting point: God is one; God is just. That is why the starting point of the theology dictates its conclusion: the deeds one does in this world bear consequences for one's situation in the world to come, and the merit attained through this-worldly deeds, for example, of generosity, persists; individuals retain their status as such through all time to come. What we see is that the issues of death and afterlife are bound up with the most fundamental concerns of Judaism: God's unity and justice (encompassing mercy). Without a doctrine of resurrection and afterlife, Judaism cannot accomplish its goals of establishing the justice of the one and only God of the world.

The other two monotheisms, Islam and Christianity, concur on the basic convictions of Judaism concerning judgment after death and resurrection of the dead who stand in judgment. All concur that martyrs for the faith are especially fortunate, though the appropriate forum for martyrdom—fighting in a holy war as against giving one's life on the cross to God—will differ from one religion to the other. The three monotheisms concur on bodily resurrection of the dead. None expresses final certainty on such questions as the fate of the body and the soul after death, but all know for certain that the body and the soul are united in the resurrection. Then each person is judged, with those justified admitted to paradise/Eden/heaven. The words differ; the intent is the same.

Where Christianity makes its particular statement, it is always in connection with the figure of Christ. To be sure, death is a radical changing in the life of a person: "the current configuration of relationships and of reality is wiped away." Death is not a punishment but an opportunity, as Bruce Chilton says. Resurrection then follows, just as Christ himself was raised from the dead. Resurrection is of the body, not only of the soul or spirit, just as Judaism and Islam maintain. All of this, in Professor Chilton's words, represents a statement concerning human regeneration: "Humanity is regarded not simply as a quality that God values, but as the very center of human being in the image of God. That center is so precious to God, it is the basis upon which it is possible for human beings to enter the kingdom of God, both now and eschatologically."

If the religions of monotheism agree on a last judgment, Indian religions concur on linking the afterlife to the life one has lived in this world.

There is a connection between religious acts of sacrifice and the results of such acts not only in this life but also in an afterlife in heaven. Brian Smith states, "This theory of moral cause and effect, sometimes referred to as 'the law of karma,' posited future existences not only in a heaven or hell but also rebirth (of various sorts) in this world, and all such rebirths were seen as correlated to one's past karma." But death is not final: "birth, life, death, and rebirth are stages in the endless cycle of existence called *samsara*." That is why, as Professor Smith notes, "for Hinduism, then, the problem is not so much death itself as it is continual, perpetual, and potentially eternal rebirth. . . . Hinduism . . . offers an alternative to the endless cycle of rebirth . . . a state of 'release' or 'liberation' from samsara, an eternal and changeless state of salvation that not only overcomes death but also frees one from continual rebirth."

If we divide the religions treated in this book into groups, the monotheist ones form one group; Hinduism and Buddhism, the other. Monotheism in the mythic versions of Judaism, Christianity, and Islam affirms life and promises eternal life beyond the grave. Hinduism and Buddhism concur that breaking the cycle of existence, attaining a state of sublimity, overcoming this world, and finding ultimate egress from it— these represent the goal of life. The five religions concur that the grave represents the focus of life, the death that comes to us all the source of wisdom and moral consciousness, the actualization of the human condition above any other event of life. But in addressing the grave, as we shall now see, each formulates its own story of life: its ultimate destination and meaning. The issues taken up in these pages turn out to bear the heaviest burden of the world religions treated in this series, and that is why, with this volume, we conclude our exposition.

We have formulated the most fundamental questions concerning death that we could imagine. Why does one die and how does one die? What happens after death? What of resurrection (for Judaism, Christianity, and Islam) and reincarnation (for Hinduism and Buddhism)? And the answers to these specific questions lead us into the deepest layers of reflection of all five religions about the meaning of a human life, the nature and destiny of human existence.

CHAPTER I

Buddhism

CHARLES HALLISEY

Some of the most important lessons to be learned from Buddhist attitudes toward death and the afterlife can be seen in a letter by Rennyo (1415–99), a great thinker and leader in the Shin (Pure Land) Buddhist tradition, a major school of Japanese Buddhism. This letter is, in fact, read at Shin Buddhist funerals and is known by heart by many Shin Buddhists:

> When we carefully contemplate the transitory aspect of human beings, we usually conclude that, that which is impermanent . . . is our life-span in this world. . . . One's period of life passes quickly and who today retains the human form for 100 years? Is it I or another that will go first; not knowing whether it is to be today or tomorrow? Life is as fragile as the beads of morning dew clustered around the base of plants and the tiny droplets hanging from the tips of their leaves. We are, therefore, beings that may have faces radiant with life in the morning, and in the evening be white ashes.
>
> No sooner than we are claimed by the wind of impermanency, our eyes are instantly closed. When that one breath can nevermore be had, the radiancy of health alters in vain and we lose the vibrance of life. Our family and relatives then gather and though they may lament in strickened sadness, there can be no altering of the situation. Not able to leave things as they are and after they escort our bodies to the outlying field to vanish as a column of smoke in the middle of the night, only white ashes remain. To say

I

that ours is a most pitiful state hardly begins to describe our true
plight.

Therefore, since the transiency of human beings is of this
world where both the old and the young alike are impermanent,
we should all make haste to place securely within our hearts the
prime importance of the life to come in a permanent world[1] and
recite the Nembutsu[2] with deep and total reliance upon Amida
Buddha.[3]

In this letter, Rennyo depicts death in a number of apparently
contradictory ways. Death is something that is unavoidable and
inevitable, but it is also something that we can escape from.
Death is something that is certain, but we can be uncertain only
about when or how we will die. Death is something that seems
to epitomize the limits of what we can know, and fills us with
fear, but it is also something that we can learn from, and thus
something we must carefully look at. Death is something that
each of us must experience in a state of radical aloneness, but it
is also something that helps us to see that this experience is the
same for everyone, and with the empathy that comes from this
realization of fundamental human sameness, we come to have
pity for others. In other words, death prompts us to develop
both wisdom and compassion—wisdom about ourselves and
about the nature of the world, and compassion for the sufferings of ourselves and others that makes us want to end such
suffering. Significantly, wisdom and compassion define the nature of a Buddha, preeminently a being who has transcended
death once and for all but who also helps others to accomplish
this themselves.

The tone of Rennyo's letter is also worth noting because
Rennyo's aesthetic stance toward death is shared with many
others in the diverse religious traditions of the Buddhist world.
Rennyo is stark in his acknowledgment of the human fragility
that is all too visible in death, and he is firm in his confidence at

being able to stare death down and to transcend ultimately its grasp. Moreover, the aesthetic qualities of starkness and firmness suggest the moral virtues of stoicism and nobility that Buddhists commonly admire in persons, but especially in those who face death with a sense of ease and of what is important. Rennyo has an understated aesthetic appreciation of our fragility too. He subtly suggests that our transience heightens the beauty of our lives with his images that we are like drops of morning dew.

A human warmth colors Rennyo's letter, which can be felt when he traces the gap between the "strickened sadness" of loved ones before an unalterable situation. Rennyo's reference to funeral practices in his letter reminds us not only that ideas about death and the afterlife are commonly affirmed, if not taught, in the midst of religious practice, but also that these practices themselves may express sentiments that exceed what is explicitly countenanced by orthodox ideas. Death is hard for the living, and in the practices associated with death, we often see how the living are, as Rennyo says, "not able to leave things as they are."

From just these brief comments on Rennyo's short letter, we can see that it is probably impossible to do justice to all that Buddhists have seen and felt in recognizing that death is both a part of human life and a foe to it and that there are states beyond death that humans can attain. We can concentrate on only a few aspects in this chapter. In the first part of this chapter, we will examine first how Buddhists have seen death as something to be learned from. We will also consider in this part how a good death prefigures the states beyond death, although these states will not be discussed until the third part of the chapter. In the second part, we will look at Buddhist ideas about what happens after death, but especially at these ideas as they are displayed in the rituals that Buddhists perform in connection with death. We will also be alert to discerning the presence of sentiments that exceed what is explicitly countenanced by orthodox ideas, sentiments that are centrally human, even if suspect Buddhistically.

Such sentiments have an acknowledged place in Buddhist communities, accepted within the tolerance of cultural diversity that has marked the Buddhist world historically. Ideas and practices associated with death exhibit as much local variation as anything else in the Buddhist world. Most Buddhists are cremated, but in some places and at some times, Buddhists have thrown the bodies of the deceased into rivers, have buried them, and have given some a "sky burial," where the body is left exposed to the natural elements. Local variation is often attributed purely to practical need; when there was no wood, then other means for disposing a body besides cremation were preferred. Ideas about what happens after death and about various kinds of afterlife are equally diverse. Differences in Buddhist thought and practice are not only between different times and places, but also between individuals living in the same community. For example, it is common throughout the Buddhist world to assume that beings experience more than one life and are reborn again and again, but some Buddhists, especially in the twentieth century, have seen little reason to affirm this assumption, even as they recognize that some of their Buddhist neighbors accept it as truth. An example can be seen in the following comments by Rev. Nakatsu Isao, a contemporary Shin Buddhist priest. They are part of an answer to a question about whether Shin Buddhists believe in a cycle of birth and death or there is only one life:

> For myself my life is only once but when my life ends, that is the Pure Land. . . . The life of delusions finishes with this life. We have no belief in transmigration, in a substantial form of rebirth. But we are told in our [scriptures] that we have been drifting in the ocean of birth-and-death since the beginning of our era (*kalpa*). . . . In household [religion] there is maybe a belief in transmigration or

rebirth, but only few believe it. We regard it as superstition if we take it as substantial.[4]

Probably more Pure Land Buddhists in particular, and more Buddhists in general, assume the truth of rebirth as a substantial reality than Rev. Isao would have us believe, but his comments are a useful reminder that a diversity of belief, practice, and sentiment is found everywhere in the Buddhist world.

At the same time there is such diversity, there is still considerable consistency in basic attitudes toward death throughout the Buddhist world, especially insofar as death is considered to be both the ultimate disvalue in human life and a proximate value in a good human life.

That death is something to be directly faced and learned from as well as something to be escaped is found just as much in the earliest layers of the tradition. The idea of death as proximate value and ultimate disvalue is a structuring theme in the biography of the Buddha himself. Traditional biographies of the Buddha portray him as the pampered son of a king who was so sheltered by his father that he did not observe, much less experience, any of the adversity and unpleasantness that ordinarily occur in every human life. The young prince was surrounded by every luxury in palaces and parks in which his father prevented him from seeing any indication of sickness, old age, and death. One day, when the future Buddha was twenty-nine years old, he asked a charioteer to take him through a park for pleasure. On the drive, he met an old man, and he asked his driver to explain this sight to him. The driver explained about old age, its inevitability and ubiquity, and told the prince that he, too, was subject to aging. Realizing the truth of the driver's explanation and being filled with fear, the prince was unable to find pleasure in the natural splendor of the park, and he returned to his palace. With time, however, his desire for pleasure returned and his melancholy eased, and he again went out with his driver into

the palace gardens. In the same manner as happened with the
sight of the old man, the prince saw a sick man and a corpse,
and each time he was debilitated by the realization that he, too,
was subject to the natural processes that caused old age, sickness, and death. On a fourth excursion, however, the future
Buddha saw an ascetic, someone who had renounced the con-
ventions of society, but more important, someone who seemed
to be serene. The chariot driver explained that this was a person
in search of "the deathless," a state beyond death, and this sight
and the driver's explanation filled the future Buddha with happiness. He resolved to become like this ascetic, and he decided
to renounce the world.

Six years later, he accomplished his goal. He "woke up," that
is, he became a Buddha, and in the moment of his enlightenment, he was aware that he had escaped from death. He exulted
in this self-awareness, exclaiming,

I ran through samsara,[5] *with its many births,*
Searching for, but not finding, the house-builder.
Misery is birth again and again.
House-builder, you are seen!
The house you shall not build again!
Broken are your rafters, all,
Your roof beam destroyed.
Freedom from the samkharas[6] *has the mind attained.*
To the end of cravings has it come.[7]

A Theravada commentary on these verses explains that the line
"Misery is birth again and again" also is about old age, sickness,
and death, the first three of the four sights that the future Buddha saw in his palace garden, because birth is the condition for
the others. The commentator goes on to connect life in this
house of death with ignorance and emphasizes that the truth
about life sets one free from death:

This statement ["Misery is birth again and again"] (gives) the reason for the search of the house builder: It is a torment to undergo this process of being born again and again, mixed up as it is with decay, disease, and death.

"You are seen" [means] now you are seen by me, as I penetrated through to the wisdom of complete enlightenment.

"The house you shall not build again" [means] no more will you build for me this house of individuality in this whirl of samsara. . . .

"Your roof beam destroyed" [means] and also destroyed by me is the pinnacle of this house of individuality that is built by you and constituted by ignorance.[8]

WHY ONE DIES AND HOW ONE DIES

The commentator's explanation of why the Buddha said that "Misery is birth again and again" on the night of his enlightenment indicates in short order that anyone would want to escape death. For the commentator, further explanation is not necessary. Death is obviously an extreme form of suffering, and the commentator, like most Buddhists, assumes that it is self-evident that no one, or at least no one in his or her right mind, would want to suffer.

But it can also be said that, even as the Buddhist life is ultimately aimed at escaping death, death occupies an essential place in a good Buddhist life. The very fact of death as an inevitable part of human life, for example, lends urgency and seriousness to religious practice, as was seen in Rennyo's admonition that "we should all make haste" to secure "the life to come in a permanent world."[9]

Understanding why we die is also part of a good life. Indeed, it is key to understanding the truth about life that will set us free from death. Buddhist explanations of why human beings die, however, are not explanations about why there is death in the first place. In this, the Buddhist traditions seem to be an exception to the general pattern found in many other religions and cultures wherein death is portrayed as something whose existence requires explanation. Buddhists seem to have felt little need for such an explanation, often dismissing such speculation as unprofitable. Death is an eternal reality in Buddhist thought, a given, and there is no time in the past when there was not death in this world, just as there was not a point when there was not life.

What does it mean, then, to understand why we die? To understand death is to understand our existence within a broader perspective, and thus to see ourselves "exactly as we are," but this is precisely the place where the diversity of Buddhist ideas about the nature of reality leaves its mark on Buddhist ideas about death. For some Buddhists, understanding why one dies means that one comes to see the givens of life and death, which cause us so much anguish, as no more real than anything else in this illusory world. Teaching that the nature of the world eludes any adequate description, the Lotus Sutra, one of the most influential Buddhist scriptures in East Asia, says that the Buddha perceives the true aspect of the threefold world exactly as it is. There is no ebb or flow of birth and death, and there is no existing in this world and later entering extinction. It is neither substantial nor empty, neither consistent nor diverse. It is not what those who dwell in the threefold world perceive it to be.[10]

For other Buddhists with a more realistic conception of the world, to understand why one dies is to see oneself as subject to unchanging natural laws, the most general of which is the impermanence of all things. A modern Theravadin writer from Thailand, Phra Payutto, explains,

> According to the basic principles of [the Buddha's teachings], all things are born of the conjoining of various elements or take form due to the composition of various elements. This does not simply mean gathering separate parts and putting them together to create

a form, such as putting various materials together to make tools. Actually, the statement that all things come into being from the conjoining of various elements is simply an expression to facilitate understanding at a basic level. In reality, all things exist in a constant flow or flux. Each and every component part comes into being due to the break up or disintegration of other component parts; and each of these parts does not have its own essence and arises and passes away one after the other in unending succession, without absolute certainty or stability. This flow continues to evolve or proceed in a way that seems to maintain a form or course because all of the component parts have a connected and interdependent causal relationship and because each component has no essence of its own and is, therefore, in constant flux.

All of this goes in accordance with nature and depends upon the relationship of combined and dependent effects; there are no other forces coming into play dependent on a creator or mysterious power. For purposes of simplicity, let us refer to this as natural law.[11]

In the Theravada school of Buddhism found in Sri Lanka and Southeast Asia, death is just another instance of impermanence. The association between death and impermanence is so deep that some Theravadin thinkers use the notion of death to refer to the constant dissolution of all conditioned phenomena.[12] Death then is only another instance of the flux that characterizes all existence, distinguished from other instances of "momentary death" because the connected and interdependent causal relationships that give the impression of a stable form over the course of time themselves change in death, with the component parts combining into some other form. To give one example crudely: our bodies do not end at death; some of our flesh becomes part of the flesh of bacteria, insects, and animals, while some of it becomes soil, its nutrients absorbed by plants. In Buddhist thought, our consciousness is among the component parts that make up our existence that similarly combine after death with new component parts to create the impression of another stable form, another life.

Both the Lotus Sutra and Payutto assume quite a lot about the nature of human beings in their redescription of death as illusory and as an instance of impermanence. Note especially, however, that neither makes any mention of a soul or any other site of permanent identity that continues through the lifetime of a person. Buddhist thought characteristically denies the existence of a soul or any permanence to a person, and this allows no space for questions of whether and how a soul survives after death.

Impermanence explains why death occurs now, why someone who is already born must die, but this natural law does not explain why there should be death in the future. The condition for death in the future is ignorance in the present, ignorance that encourages us to act as if we were exceptions to the rule of the natural order of things. The role of ignorance in creating the necessary conditions for death was systematically presented by the Buddha in the law of dependent co-origination (*paticcasamuppada*). In the following sermon, the Buddha is describing the career of a previous Buddha, Vipassi, before he had attained enlightenment and was still a future Buddha (Bodhisatta):

Now there arose in the mind of Vipassi, when he had gone to his place and was meditating in seclusion, the following consideration: "Truly this world has fallen upon trouble; one is born, and grows old, and dies, and falls from one state, and is reborn in another."

"And from this suffering, moreover, no one knows of any way of escape, even from decay and death. O when shall a way of escape from this suffering be made known, from decay and from death!"

Then to Vipassi, this thought occurred: "What now being

present, is decay and death also present; what conditions decay and dying?" Then from attention to the cause arose the conviction through reason: "Where birth is, there is decay and dying; birth is the condition of decay and dying."[13]

The Buddha goes on to tell how Vipassi examines the condition for birth and finds it to be "becoming," or as Payutto explains, the "purposeful action that leads to existence and continuing on according to our attachments."[14] In turn, the condition for this purposeful action is attachment, which in turn is made possible by craving. Craving can occur when there are evaluative feelings; when we have a pleasant sensation, we desire to have more of it. Sensation's condition is the processes of sensory experience. Sensory experience is possible when there are senses; according to Buddhist thought, there are six senses: eyes, ears, nose, tongue, body, and the mind (the mind is a sense organ in that there are sensory experiences that we have strictly through the mind, such as angst). The conditions for the senses are the constituent elements of an embodied person, both bodily and psychological. Consciousness is the condition for the existence of the embodied person.

There are a number of versions of the law of dependent co-origination in Buddhist scriptures. The version attributed to Vipassi had ten elements and ended with consciousness. Frequently, the Buddha added two further conditions to this chain of causation, and this is the most authoritative account. The two additional elements are the *samkharas*[15] and ignorance. The *samkharas* were mentioned in the verses of happiness that the Buddha uttered on the night of his enlightenment; they are mental and moral predispositions, such as pessimism and optimism, that shape one's experience of the world. Ignorance, however, is the root cause of them all, and thus ultimately, ignorance is the necessary condition for death. The chain of causation can be presented in the following fashion:

With ignorance as condition there arise
- *samkharas*
- consciousness
- embodied personality
- the six senses
- sensory experience
- evaluative feelings
- craving
- becoming
- birth

- *samkharas*
- consciousness
- embodied personality
- the six senses
- sensory experience
- evaluative feelings
- craving
- becoming
- birth
- decay and death[16]

This schema of dependent co-origination was often depicted as a circle, with decay and death, in turn, serving as the condition for the arising of ignorance. This allowed the account to suggest how the Wheel of Life, the cycle of birth, death, and rebirth in this world, turns with ignorance as its hub, holding all the other elements of existence together as the root cause of their existence: "It is the beginningless round of rebirths that is called the 'Wheel of the round of rebirths.' Ignorance is its hub because it is its root. Aging-and-death is its rim because it terminates it. The remaining ten states [of the dependent co-origination] are its spokes because ignorance is their root and aging-and-death their termination."[17]

Impermanence and ignorance are necessary elements in any adequate explanation of death, but they are not sufficient. They do not explain, for example, why one person dies asleep in her bed in old age, while another dies young under the most tragic circumstances. To understand why we die is to understand why we die in a particular manner. Impermanence and ignorance are the conditions for death in general, but if we are to understand why we die in different ways, we must turn elsewhere.

The story of the death of Mahamoggallana, one of the greatest disciples of the Buddha, suggests where we should turn. Moggallana was preeminent among the Buddha's disciples in

many of his religious accomplishments. He had become enlightened only a week after first being instructed by the Buddha
and was recognized by the Buddha himself for his teaching
skills. The circumstances of his death, however, seemed to be in
striking contrast to the accomplishments of his life. He was
murdered by thieves who "tore him limb from limb, and
pounded his bones until they were as small as grains of rice."[18]
When his fellow monks learned of the cruel way in which he
was killed, they said,

> "Elder Moggallana the Great met death which he did not de-
> serve." At that moment the Teacher [i.e., the Buddha] approached
> and asked them, "Monks, what are you saying as you sit here all
> gathered together?" When they told him, he said, "Monks, if you
> regard only this present state of existence, Moggallana the Great
> did indeed meet death which he did not deserve. But as a matter of
> fact, the manner of death he met was in exact conformity with the
> deed he committed in a previous state of existence."[19]

When the monks asked what Moggallana had done that made
him deserve such a death, the Buddha told a story about how
Moggallana had murdered his blind parents in a previous life by
beating them to death while pretending to be a thief, and concluded, "Monks, by reason of the fact that Moggallana committed so monstrous a sin, he suffered torment for numberless
hundreds of thousands of years in Hell; and thereafter, because
the fruit of his evil deed was not yet exhausted, in a hundred
successive existences he was beaten and pounded to pieces in
like manner and so met death. Therefore the manner of death
which Moggallana suffered was in exact conformity with his
own misdeed in a previous state of existence."[20]

The Buddha explains the shocking circumstances of Moggallana's death in terms of *karma,* the law of moral cause and
effect. As the tit-for-tat quality of the story of Moggallana's

death makes clear, under the law of karma a bad action produces a like result, just as a good action produces a good result. Thus to explain why one dies in a particular manner, it is necessary to understand the workings of karma in the world.

With respect to karma, however, the proximate value of death is not only cognitive. Differences in the circumstances of death help us to reaffirm that karma is true, and living with an awareness of karma is necessary to any good life; if we understand the nature of karma, we can see what the future will bring by looking at our actions in the present as the causes of future conditions for life and death. But karma has another proximate value in a good life, as the Buddha's story about Moggallana makes clear. His cruel murder of his parents had an excessive fruit: he suffered in hell for an unimaginable time, but even then "the fruit of his evil deed was not yet exhausted." Death is a way of lessening karmic retribution and makes it unnecessary for more suffering to occur in the future.

Understanding why one dies changes how one dies. That was even the case with Moggallana. He was skilled in various occult powers, and thus through clairvoyance, he was aware of the thieves' schemes to murder him. We are told in the story about his death that at first he eluded the thieves by using his magical powers to change his shape and to fly through the air. But after three months of keeping one step ahead of the thieves, he "felt the compelling force of the evil deed he himself committed in a previous state of existence, and made no attempt to get away."[21] The ability to know the specifics of karma, as Moggallana did, is a rare accomplishment, but even more general understandings of why one dies change how one dies.

Daisaku Ikeda, the leader of Soka Gakkai International,[22] a movement that originated in Japan in this century, gives an example of how understanding why one dies changes how one reacts to death:

On 12 August 1985 a Japan Air Lines jumbo jet crashed in the mountain north of Tokyo, and 520 people lost their lives. I heard the news with great sadness, and prayed for the victims. . . . The husband and parents of one of the crash victims, all of whom practise Nichiren Daishonin's Buddhism, have written to me and reported that, while originally they bitterly regretted the tragedy, they have since become able to confront the situation face to face and use it to strengthen their faith. . . . They have been able to do this because they have increased their understanding of what Buddhism teaches about how one can lessen the retribution of one's negative karma through experiencing such tragedies.[23]

Phra Payutto gives yet another way that understanding the general conditions for why one dies has proximate value in a good life:

In terms of internal aspects or direct psychological benefits, the principle of impermanence helps us to live with a mind that can keep pace with the truth. . . .

At the basic levels of ethics, the principle of impermanence teaches us to know the common nature of things. This knowledge keeps [suffering] within limits when degeneration or loss takes place. . . . At higher levels, the principle of impermanence teaches us to gradually attain truth . . . ; it allows us to live with a free mind, free from attachments and [suffering]. This is called living with total and true mental health.

The principle of impermanence is often used as a means of calming yourself or others when disaster, suffering, or loss occurs. It can be more or less consoling.[24]

Whether one sees death as illusory, as an instance of the workings of karma, or as an instance of the natural law of impermanence, one comes to have an awareness of the way things are, with respect both to the world and to oneself. This awareness changes how one experiences death, allowing one to face death with equanimity rather than fear, with acceptance rather than a vain struggle to escape. The *Dhammapada,* a collection of sayings attributed to the Buddha, says that "they who are aware do not die," and the commentary of this expression explains,

> It should not be considered that [those who are aware—that is, beings who are endowed with mindfulness of the nature of reality] become (literally) freed of decay and death. There is of course no being who is beyond death and decay. (What is meant is that) for the unaware the whirl (i.e. the round of births and deaths) is unbroken; for one with awareness it is broken. Hence, because the unaware are not liberated from birth, and so forth, they are said to be dead, whether (factually) dead or alive.
>
> Those who are aware, having developed the characteristic of awareness, in a short time [become enlightened], and do not take birth in a second or third life. Hence, they, whether living or dead, do not, indeed, die.[25]

The presence of awareness is key to deciding what is a good death, as can be seen in the case of suicide. There is an account in the Theravada canon of a monk named Channa who "was a sick man, in pain, grievously ill."[26] Because he could not stand the pain, he decided to commit suicide, saying, "I am not getting better, I am not keeping going; my grievously painful feelings are increasing, not lessening; an increase in them is apparent, not a lessening. I will take a knife (to myself), I do not desire life."[27] Other monks tried to prevent him from taking his own life, thinking that he felt that way because he lacked food, medicine, and care, but when they saw that he could not be dissuaded, they questioned him about his awareness of the nature of the world, trying to discover whether his intention was prompted by a misguided view. They found that he was fully aware that there was no soul or permanent self that could somehow escape its painful circumstances in the present through suicide, and they reminded him of the Buddha's teaching that the craving for future existence was the cause of birth and thus the condition for death again in the future. Channa subsequently committed suicide, and when the Buddha was told about the event, he said that Channa was to be blamed for his action. There was no fault in it because Channa did not have any desire for existence in the face of death, as expressed in his ability to master his fear of dying at the moment of death. "But whoever lays down this body and grasps after another body, of him I say he is to be blamed."[28]

In the Buddhist view, then, good death is distinguished by one's state of mind, by volitional and affective factors, at the moment of death, and not by outward circumstances. A good death is one that bears the fruit of a lifetime of religious practice, practices that have corrected the volitional and affective predisposition through which we experience the world. It will be one in which the dying person is aware of the way things are, not afraid, at ease, and in a state of serenity, as can be seen in the following assurances found in the Pure Land Sutras:

> Some living beings will bring to mind the [Buddha], envisioning him again and again with all his characteristics, and they will plant many and limitless roots of merit, and they will dedicate their thoughts to awakening, vowing to be reborn in Amitabha's Land of Bliss. When the time of their death approaches, the [Buddha], the perfectly and fully awakened Amitabha will stand before these beings, and he will appear surrounded and honored by a host of countless monks. Thereupon, having seen the Blessed One, their thoughts will only be thoughts of serene trust, and forthwith they will be reborn in the Land of Bliss.[29]

WHAT HAPPENS AFTER DEATH

Although Buddhist discussions about why one dies make it clear that death should be seen from the perspective of larger and more general processes, it is important to focus more closely on death as a unique part of a person's life. In the contemporary world, we may debate whether the absence of mental activity constitutes death (i.e., brain death), or the cessation of breathing or of the heart beating. Buddhists traditionally tended to define death in terms of a person as a combination of component parts: as soon as the body is no longer able to support psychological processes, especially consciousness, there is death.

Buddhists have been particularly interested in what happens immediately before this moment as well as what happens after it. Their concerns about what happens immediately before and after death with respect to the bodily and spiritual aspects of a person help us to see what they consider to be important about the more long-term afterlife of a person.

Dying is not the same as death. For many Buddhist traditions, dying is, strictly speaking, not a moment, but a process with its own stages. These involve the gradual withdrawal of consciousness from the senses, the stopping of breathing, and the decay of the body, and there is much technical description of these stages in Buddhist scholastic literature.[30]

The decay of the body is the first thing that one can see after death: "a body one day dead or two days dead, or three days dead, swollen, blue and festering."[31] Tibetan Buddhist medicine looks for more subtle signs of decay as a mark of death having occurred. Medical discussions in Tibet, according to the Dalai Lama, sometimes focus

> on the energy center at the heart, in which there are said to be a very subtle white element and a red element. In the process of dying, the white element descends from the head, down through the

central channel, and then stops at the heart center. From below the heart a very subtle red element, or drop, arises. As the very subtle white element descends to the heart, one has the experience of a pale light. Following this, the red element ascends to the heart, and while this is occurring, there is a subjective experience of a reddish sheen arising. When the two completely converge, like two bowls coming together, there is a period of blackout, as if one loses consciousness altogether. Following that blackout period is the period of the clear light of death.

The clear light of death is something that everyone, without exception, experiences, but there is much variation in terms of how long the experience is sustained. For some people it may last only a few seconds; for some, a few minutes; for some, several days or even weeks. As long as the clear light of death experience is sustained, the connection between the subtle energy-mind and the gross physical body has not been severed. It is in the process of being severed, but it has not been completely severed. At the very moment that the severance takes place, the body begins to decay, and at that point we say death has occurred. The external sign of this taking place, by means of which one can know with full certainty that death has taken place, is that these red and white elements emerge from the nostrils. This is seen as a red trace and a white trace, which may also be emitted from the genitals. This is true for both men and women.[32]

When the body and the components of the conscious life lose their causal connection, the basis of the latter, what the Dalai Lama called above our "energy-mind," enters into an "intermediate state" between death and the next rebirth. This intermediate state is subject to considerable speculation; consequently, there is considerable diversity among Buddhist thinkers about its length, its nature, and what can happen to an individual while in it. Relatively little attention is given to this intermediate state in the Theravada tradition of Sri Lanka and Southeast Asia, aside from specifying its length as lasting from seven days to seven weeks.

The Tibetan *Book of the Dead* gives what is perhaps the most elaborate account of this intermediate disembodied state between death and rebirth known in Tibetan Buddhism as the *bardo,* and in its detail, it is typical of the kind of reflection about what happens after death that is found in the Mahayana traditions of Tibet and East Asia.

The *Book of the Dead* specifies three stages in passing through this state. This first gives the consciousness of a dying person an opportunity to fuse with and be incorporated into absolute "suchness" of the universe, with an abandonment of all elements of self-consciousness and personal identification. For a few, this experience will be the consummation of existence, and they will remain perpetually in this state. For most, however, karma and cravings for existence at the end of the previous life will draw them away from this perfect state beyond birth and death.

They will enter a second stage, in which consciousness takes on a mentally created body mirroring the physical body that it once had. Various Buddhas appear to this consciousness then, and in each case, the person can identify with this Buddha and attain a state of spiritual oneness with it. When this occurs, the consciousness remains in this state as a future Buddha with conditions that are ideal for total enlightenment and escape from death. For many people, feelings of distance and disidentification occur when these Buddhas appear because of an awareness of their own faults or because they still crave existence in the world; they will be subsequently reborn in a lower realm. After the Buddhas appear, terrifying apparitions appear. When the consciousness takes them as real, and not as projections of a continuing moral nature, these apparitions become real to the person, binding the dead person to subsequent existence in the world.

In the third stage, the consciousness assumes a physical, albeit subtle, body. This embodied consciousness tries to reenter its previous body, but doing this proves impossible. This person is then judged by the lord of death according to its actions in its previous life. "It sees its good and evil deeds weighed, and feels itself racked and hacked by demons. Since its body is a mental projection, it is not destroyed, but continues to feel the self-punishments as long as it adheres to and projects the reality of that body and its sins. At last it is released, only to be pursued by furies across many strange landscapes prior to material rebirth."[33]

Many Buddhists explicitly think that while a deceased person is in this intermediate state, its future can be affected by actions on its behalf by those it left behind. These efforts are places where we see, as Rennyo says, that people who loved the deceased are "not able to leave things as they are" but, even after death, look for ways to show their care and concern for a loved one.

In Sri Lanka, a family organizes a ritual gift of food for monks on the seventh day after death. After they are fed, the monks affirm that what has been given will benefit the dead, saying, "As the full water-bearing (rivers) fill the ocean, so indeed does what is given here benefit the dead."[34] The monks then give a sermon that usually focuses on the truth of impermanence. Following the sermon, the merit of all of these actions, both the feeding of the monks and the listening to the sermon, is transferred to the dead person, and a member of the family says, "May this be for my relatives. May my relatives be happy."[35] This merit presumably will help the deceased attain a better state in the next rebirth, although Theravada doctrine about merit and individual responsibility prevents this from being explicitly acknowledged.

There are no such qualms in Chinese Buddhism, traditions that are part of the Mahayana. According to one text, *The Scripture on Rebirth in Accordance with One's Vows in the Pure Lands of the Ten Directions,* good actions by others can help a person in the intermediate state between death and rebirth and steer one toward the path to enlightenment and escape from death.

> Whether one's life span has not yet ended or whether it has already passed or even on the day it ends, parents, relatives, associates, and friends can, on behalf of the one whose life span has ended, cultivate various acts of blessing. They should fast and observe the precepts with a single mind, wash and purify the body, and put on fresh, clean clothes. With one mind, they should reverence the Buddhas of the Ten Directions. They should also offer flowers and incense to the various Buddhas. If they do, then the deceased will achieve deliverance from the troubles of suffering, be raised up to heaven, and attain the way of *nirvana.*[36]

Another Chinese text, *The Scripture on Karmic Retribution,* also recommends the kind of memorial service found throughout the Buddhist world, as we saw above in an example from Sri Lanka: "Thus at death, during the first seven, the second seven, up to the seventh seven and the one hundredth day, relatives of the deceased should hold services of deliverance so the deceased will be reborn in a good place and be able to experience happiness. Making this merit is most essential."[37]

In Tibet, in addition to rituals like those found in Sri Lanka and China, in which merit is made to be transferred to a dead person, it is thought that a spiritually advanced person can directly help the deceased, either by guiding him or her through the difficult paths of the bardo, the intermediate state, giving appropriate advice and encouragement, or by carrying out rituals that effect a change in the spiritual character of the deceased.

An example of the latter can be seen in the following excerpts of ritual instructions from a Tibetan text called *The Tantra of the Sun and Moon's Intimate Union:*

> *When the person ultimately dies,*
> *You should place a vase on the crown*
> *of her defiled body,*
> *Purifying her corpse with the syllabic particle* a
> *And a flow of gnostic water.*
> *You thus eliminate the possibility of her rebirth in hell,*
> *Such that the signs are similarly (lead away upwards).*

For one evidencing signs of rebirth as a starving spirit:

> *With contemplation of the syllable* bhya
> *You intone it seven times with your breath,*
> *Place the* bhya *on her tongue in visualization,*
> *And gather in her psyche's essence by means of it;*
> *Similarly with the vase above her mouth,*
> *You give ablution with a flow of gnostic water.*
> *Having thus eliminated the possibility of rebirth as a starving spirit,*
> *That person as well is led upward.*[38]

REBIRTH IN THE SIX REALMS, REBIRTH IN THE PURE LAND, AND NIRVANA

The *Tantra of the Sun and Moon's Intimate Union* continues with ritual instructions for changing the rebirth-destiny of a person moving toward birth among animals, human beings, demigods, and gods. Together with the denizens of hell and starving spirits, these form six realms of potential rebirth that make up the cycle of birth and death in samsara. After the time in the intermediate state, each being is reborn in one of the states according to the fruits of actions done in previous lives:

"Beings reap the fruit of actions—good or bad—which they themselves have done (there is no other doer) with their body, speech, and mind."

Thus thinking, the compassionate Teacher [i.e., the Buddha], master of the Triple World, proclaimed, for the sake of all beings, which acts had which fruits.[39]

Elaborating the different conditions of rebirth in these various realms was a favorite topic for Buddhist writers, and whole works were devoted to detailing the pleasures and pains inherent in each, and which actions caused rebirth there. The following example, focusing on rebirth among human beings, gives some idea of the flavor of such works; they are obviously in the same spirit as the Buddha's explanation of Moggallana's death that we considered above:

Among gods, demigods, and humans, nonviolence leads to a long life; violence gives rise to a short life. Thus, one should abstain from violence.

Leprosy, consumption, fever, madness, and other human diseases are due to killing, tying up, and whipping creatures.

People who steal others' property and give away nothing whatsoever will never themselves become wealthy, strive as they may.

One who takes goods that were not given but who also gives gifts will, after death, first become wealthy but then exceedingly poor.

One who neither steals nor gives nor is excessively niggardly will, with great effort, obtain a lasting fortune in the next life.

People who do not steal others' property, who are generous and free from greed, obtain what they wish: great wealth that cannot be taken away.

One who, in this world, makes donations of alms food will be reborn ever-happy: endowed with long life, good complexion, strength, good fortune, and good health. . . .

He who abstains from the wives of others will obtain the wives he desires; and he who stays away from his own wives, when the place and time are not right, will again be born as a man.

The man who does not restrain his thoughts and unites with the wives of others, or finds delight in illicit parts of the body, will be reborn as a woman.

But the woman who is of good morals and little passion, who abhors her femaleness and constantly aspires to masculinity, will be reborn as a man.

All karmic rewards resemble the acts of which they are the natural outcome: suffering from sin, happiness from good deeds, and a mixture of the two from a mixed deed.[40]

All karmic rewards are also impermanent, like everything else in samsara. Rebirth in any of the six realms inevitably means death since, as we have already seen, birth is the necessary condition for death. In the Buddhist view of the universe, wherever there is birth, there will always be death. The denizens of hell and the gods in the most pleasurable heavens all experience it, just as inevitably as humans do. Thus, birth in any of these six realms is, in the end, unsatisfactory, and not an end to death.

We have already seen that Buddhists have perceived that an end to death is possible. This can occur only through enlightenment, but there has been considerable disagreement about where and how enlightenment can occur.

One answer to such questions is the Pure Land of a Buddha, such as Amitabha. In this conception of the Buddhist life, there are two paths of Buddhist practice: one can follow a long and gradual path in which one cultivates the various attributes and attainments necessary to become a Buddha, or one can take advantage of the assistance offered by a great Buddha and be reborn in the land of bliss that he has created and attain enlightenment effortlessly in one's next life. As the following account of Amitabha's western paradise makes clear, existence in that realm is characterized by happiness and pleasure. The excerpt is taken from one of the Pure Land scriptures, and the Buddha is speaking:

> Why do they call that world the land of bliss? Because in that world beings do not experience suffering, neither with their body nor with their mind, and the things that cause happiness are innumerable. . . .
>
> [That land of bliss] is adorned and enclosed by seven railings, seven rows of palm trees and strings of bells. And it is beautiful and embellished with four kinds of precious materials: gold, silver, lapis lazuli, and crystal. . . . There are lotus pools made of seven precious materials: gold, silver, lapis lazuli, crystal, red pearls, diamonds, and coral . . . and all around the lotus pools jewel-trees are growing, beautiful, and embellished with seven precious materials. . . . And in those lotus pools, lotuses are growing: various kinds of blue ones, and various kinds of yellow ones, and various kinds of red ones, and various kinds of white ones, beautiful, beautifully colored, beautifully resplendent, beautiful to look at, and as big around as the wheel of a cart. . . .
>
> Furthermore, in that Buddha field, divine musical instruments are always playing, and the earth is pleasant and golden colored. And in that Buddha field, three times each day, showers of flowers fall. . . . And the beings there, during the time it takes to eat one morning meal, can pay homage to a hundred thousand billion Buddhas, by going to other universes. And after showering each [Buddha] with a hundred thousand billion flowers, they return to their own world in time for a nap.[41]

The tone of this account is obviously mythological and probably is ill-matched to modern sensibilities. It draws on imagery common in Buddhist literature about the pleasures of the heavens, and like the realms of the gods, it is filled with abundance and ease. The beauty of this land of bliss is, like the heavens, "artificial": jeweled trees, constructed lotus ponds. Such details encourage us to see in the gaudy descriptions an underlying theme: there is a thoroughgoing opposition between life in this world and the afterlife in the land of bliss. This world is natural, while that one is constructed by effort. This world is filled with suffering of every kind, while that world is characterized by happiness. This world is transitory, while that one is permanent. The afterlife in the land of bliss is thus not a continuation of life in this world—that is found in rebirth in the six realms—but a rupture to the continuity of life here. Only with such a rupture is an escape from death possible.

Surprisingly, however, given such mythological descriptions of the land of bliss, it is also common for believers in Amitabha's Pure Land to insist that the efficacy of Amitabha's efforts occurs in this world, not after birth in his Pure Land. Rev. Isao, for example, says that Shin Buddhism

> does not teach that we become [a Buddha] after death. The problem is the salvation of the people who are living now. . . . "The person who lives true *shinjin* [faith] . . . abides in the stage of the truly settled, for he has already been grasped, never to be abandoned. There is no need to wait in anticipation for the moment of death, no need to rely on Amida's coming. At the time faith becomes settled, birth too becomes settled" (from Shinran, the founder of the Shin school of Buddhism).
>
> The stage of the truly settled is also called "no retrogression into present life." This means we don't retrogress to the life of delusion again, but "we are assured of reaching buddhahood" (Shinran).[42]

A similar pattern is found in the notion of *nirvana:* life in this world is in radical opposition to nirvana, but the experience of nirvana is, at the same time, possible while still living in this world. Nirvana literally means "blown out," and it refers to the blowing out of our inherent predispositions to do actions that create the conditions for birth and death. If this world is characterized by impermanence and flux, by things causing and being caused by each other, nirvana is characterized by permanence and stability, and it has no cause. Life in this world must always end in death, while there is no death in nirvana. If this world is the site of suffering, then nirvana is describable as happiness, as is clear in the following exchange between a Buddhist monk and a king about the nature of nirvana:

> The king asked: "Is cessation Nirvana?"—"Yes, your majesty!"— "How is that, Nagasena?"—"All the foolish common people take delight in the senses and their objects, are impressed by them, are attached to them. In that way they are carried away by the flood, and are not free from birth, old age, and death, from grief, lamentation, pain, sadness, and despair—they are, I say, not free from suffering. But the well-informed holy disciples do not take delight in the senses and their objects, are not impressed by them, are not attached to them, and in consequence their craving ceases; the cessation of craving leads successively to that of grasping, of becoming, of birth, of old age and death, of grief, lamentation, pain, sadness, and despair—that is to say to the cessation of all this mass of ill. It is thus that cessation is Nirvana."—"Very good, Nagasena!" . . .
>
> The king asked: "Do those who have not won Nirvana know how happy a state it is?"—"Yes, they do."—"But how can one know this about Nirvana without having attained it?"—"Now what do you think, your majesty? Do those who have not had their hands and feet cut off know how bad it is to have them cut off?"—"Yes, they do."—"And how do they know it?"—"From hearing the sound of the lamentations of those whose hands and feet have been cut off."—"So it is by hearing the words of those who have seen Nirvana that one knows it to be a happy state."— "Very good, Nagasena."

King Milinda said: "I will grant you, Nagasena, that Nirvana is absolute ease, and that nevertheless one cannot point to its form or shape, its duration or size, either by simile or explanation, by reason or by argument. But is there perhaps some quality of Nirvana which it shares with other things, and which lends itself to a metaphorical explanation?"—"Its form, O king, cannot be elucidated by similes, but its qualities can. . . . Nirvana shares one quality with the lotus, two with water, three with medicine. . . . As the lotus is unstained by water, so is Nirvana unstained by all the defilements. As cool water allays feverish heat, so also is Nirvana cool and allays the fever of all the passions. Moreover, as water removes the thirst of men and beasts who are exhausted, parched, thirsty, and overpowered by heat, so also Nirvana removes the craving for sensuous enjoyments, the craving for further becoming, the craving for the cessation of becoming. As medicine protects from the torments of poison, so Nirvana from the torments of poisonous passions. Moreover, as medicine puts an end to sickness, so Nirvana to all sufferings. Finally, medicine and Nirvana both give security."[43]

Rennyo, in the letter with which we began this chapter, said, "To say that ours is a most pitiful state hardly begins to describe our true plight." Part of our pitiful state is that our inevitable end is death, with all the sorrows and sufferings that it entails. Equally part of our pitiful state is that we all do easily and unwittingly get more life. Through our desires and our consequent actions, we are reborn again and again in the various conditions of this world, and with each birth, we again get death. The real afterlife, in the Buddhist traditions, is that which is an escape from death once and for all, an escape that comes with enlightenment. And paradoxically, this real afterlife is something that takes place in this life with the help of death.

CHAPTER 2

Judaism

JACOB NEUSNER

WHY ONE DIES AND HOW ONE DIES

A well-crafted religious system, such as each of the five great religions set forth in these volumes, will say the same thing about many things, and certainly, when Judaism speaks about death, the message proves wholly coherent with what the faith has to say about every other critical topic in human existence. Death and the afterlife in the Judaism of the dual Torah join together the holy community and the individual; the account of what happens to each one who dies takes on meaning only in the picture of what happens to humanity in its embodiment within Israel, God's people. Death forms the final chapter of life "in this world" and the opening page of life "in the world to come." In no way is death evil or unnatural, a penalty exacted for sin. True, death before one's time, understood in the oral Torah to be sixty years, is deemed "extirpation," that is, premature death, and under some circumstances is deemed penalty for sin. But the natural course of life, to seventy or even eighty years, represents how God made us and what God wants for us. The Judaic view of death and why we die is set forth in the following passage:[1]

> In the Torah belonging to R. Meir people found written, "And behold, it was very good" (Gen. 1:31) [means] "And behold, death is good." [The play is on the letters shared by the words "very," M'WD, and "death," MWT.]

Said R. Samuel bar Nahman, "I was riding on my grandfather's shoulder, going up from my town to Kefar Hana through Bet Shean, and I heard R. Simeon b. R. Eleazar in session and expounding in the name of R. Meir, "'And behold, it was very good'—'And behold, death is good.'"

Hama bar Hanina and R. Jonathan:

Hama bar Hanina said, "The first man (Adam) was worthy not to have to taste the taste of death. And why was the penalty of death applied to him? The Holy One, blessed be he, foresaw that Nebuchadnezzar and Hiram were destined to turn themselves into gods. Therefore the penalty of having to die was imposed upon man. That is in line with this verse of Scripture: 'You were in Eden, the garden of God' (Ez. 28:13). And was Hiram actually in Eden? But he said to him, 'You are the one who caused that one in Eden to have to die.'"

Said R. Jonathan to him, "If so, God should have decreed death only for the wicked, but not for the righteous. Rather, it was so that the wicked should not be able hypocritically to pretend to repent, so that they should not have occasion to say, 'Are not the righteous living on and on? It is only because they form a treasure of merit accruing on account of the practice of doing religious duties as well as good deeds. We too shall lay up a treasure of merit accruing from doing religious duties and good deeds.' What would come out is that the things they do would not be done sincerely, [for their own sake, but only for the sake of gaining merit]. [That is what is good about death. It prevents the wicked from perverting the holy life by doing the right thing for the wrong reason. Everyone dies, so there is no point in doing religious duties only so as to avoid dying.]"

R. Yohanan and R. Simeon b. Laqish:

R. Yohanan said, "On what account was a decree of death issued against the wicked? It is because, so long as the wicked live,

they anger the Holy One, blessed be he. That is in line with the
following verse of Scripture: 'You have wearied the Lord with your
deeds' (Mal. 2:17). When they die, they stop angering the Holy
One, blessed be he. That is in line with the following verse of
Scripture: 'There the wicked cease from raging' (Job 3:17). There
the wicked cease angering the Holy One, blessed be he.

"On what account, however, is the decree of death issued
against the righteous? It is because so long as the righteous live,
they have to conduct warfare against their impulse to do evil.
When they die, they find rest. That is in line with this verse: 'And
there the weary are at rest' (Job 3:17). 'It is enough, we have labored
long enough.'"

Simeon b. Laqish said, "It is so as to give an ample reward for
the one, and to exact ample punishment from the other. To give
ample reward to the righteous, who really never were worthy of
having to taste the taste of death but accepted the taste of death
for themselves. Therefore: 'in their land they shall possess double'
(Is. 61:7).

"'And to exact ample punishment from the wicked,' for the
righteous had not been worthy of having to taste the taste of death
but they had accepted the taste of death for themselves on account
[of the wicked]. Therefore: 'And destroy them with a double destruction' (Jer. 17:18)."

—Genesis Rabbah IX:V.1–3

Through life, the righteous struggle against their impulse to do
evil; death ends the struggle and opens the way to a life of peace
and contentment. For this Judaism maintains that when we die,
we go on to "the world to come," "the Garden of Eden," "the
Heavenly academy," or in the other direction, to Gehenna, but
only for a spell. That is until the Messiah comes and the dead
are raised. But since the Messiah comes to save Israel, the resurrection of the dead forms a chapter in the salvation of the community. Therefore, we have to allow the Torah as our sages teach

it to outline its views of matters, rather than bringing a set of questions that do not correspond in proportion to the issues of death and afterlife as they are set forth by the dual Torah. Matters begin with how we die, and predictably, sages' manner of dying, comparable in context to Jesus' passion on the cross, provides the model for how humanity attains a good death.

We see once more that what the Judaic religious system stated in the Torah, oral and written, says about one subject, it says about every other subject. Critical to the system as a whole are the categories of Torah, God revealed through the Torah, and Israel called into being to receive the Torah. Hence, death too is represented in the context of the Torah and of Israel, the supernatural community. The issues concerning death take shape around considerations critical to the Torah, that is, how the righteous die, how the wicked die. And it must follow, for the oral Torah, the death of the sages, masters of the Torah, will convey the message that the system at every point proposes to set forth.

The sages of the oral Torah, accordingly, exemplify a good death.[2] What this means at its essential point is simple: the Torah calls on humanity to exercise free will by obeying God's Torah, and sin results from arrogance, virtue from humility. The story of the human condition, from the creation of Man and Woman forward, is the tale of the struggle between humanity and the passionate, commanding God, who has created humanity. The struggle arises because humanity has free will to obey and love God or to disobey and defy God. How this plays itself out in connection with the death of sages presents no surprises: the great sage dies at a moment of humility before God, on the one side, and of Torah-study, on the other. We first consider the good death as a moment in the midst of Torah-study, and in the next section, the good death as a statement of humility.

It follows that the death stories are told under the aspect of the Torah and show the supernatural power of the Torah to transform even the moment of death into an occasion of Torah-learning. We start with the tale of how a sage coped with the death of a loved one had to draw into alignment with how a sage studied the Torah; the Torah obviously provided the model of the correct confrontation. How a sage died—the death scene, with its quiet lessons—likewise presented a model for others. The encounter with death took narrative shape in the account of how the sage accepted comfort:

When the son of Rabban Yohanan ben Zakkai died, his disciples came in to bring him comfort.

R. Eliezer came in and took a seat before him and said to him, "My lord, with your permission, may I say something before you."

He said to him, "Speak."

He said to him, "The first Man had a son who died, and he accepted comfort in his regard. And how do we know that he accepted comfort in his regard?

"As it is said, And Adam knew his wife again (Gen. 4:25). You, too, be comforted."

Said he to him, "Is it not enough for me that I am distressed on my own account, that you should mention to me the distress of the first Man?"

R. Joshua came in and said to him, "My lord, with your permission, may I say something before you."

He said to him, "Speak."

He said to him, "Job had sons and daughters who died, and he accepted comfort in their regard. And how do we know that he accepted comfort in their regard?

"As it is said, *'The Lord gave and the Lord has taken away, blessed be the name of the Lord'* (Job 1:21). You, too, be comforted."

Said he to him, "Is it not enough for me that I am distressed on my own account, that you should mention to me the distress of Job?"

R. Yosé came in and took a seat before him and said to him, "My lord, with your permission, may I say something before you."

He said to him, "Speak."

He said to him, "Aaron had two grown-up sons who died on the same day, and he accepted comfort in their regard.

"For it is said, *'And Aaron held his peace'* (Lev. 10:3), and silence means only comfort. You, too, be comforted."

Said he to him, "Is it not enough for me that I am distressed on my own account, that you should mention to me the distress of Aaron?"

R. Simeon came in and said to him, "My lord, with your permission, may I say something before you."

He said to him, "Speak."

He said to him, "King David had a son who died, and he accepted comfort in his regard. You, too, be comforted. And how do we know that he accepted comfort in his regard?

"As it is said, *'And David comforted Bath Sheba his wife and went in unto her and lay with her and she bore a son and called his name Solomon'* (2 Sam. 12:24). You, too, be comforted."

Said he to him, "Is it not enough for me that I am distressed on my own account, that you should mention to me the distress of King David?"

R. Eleazar b. Arakh came in. When he saw him, he said to his servant, "Take my clothes and follow me to the bathhouse [so that I can prepare to accept consolation], for he is a great man and I shall not be able to resist his arguments."

He came in and took a seat before him and said to him, "I shall draw a parable for you. To what may the matter be compared? To the case of a man with whom the king entrusted a treasure. Every day he would weep and cry saying, 'Woe is me, when shall I get complete and final relief from this treasure that has been entrusted to me.'

"You, too, my lord, had a son, he recited from the Torah, Prophets and Writings, Mishnah, laws, lore, and has departed from this world without sin. You have reason, therefore, to accept consolation for yourself that you have returned your treasure, entrusted to you, whole and complete."

He said to him, "R. Eleazar b. Arakh, my son, you have given comfort to me in the right way in which people console one another."

— *The Fathers according to Rabbi Nathan* XIV:IV.1

The first four disciples, Eliezer, Joshua, Yosé, and Simeon, all invoke biblical models. Scripture is insufficient. Eleazar then presents an argument resting on the oral Torah: the son had studied the Torah, inclusive of the Mishnah, laws, and lore. He departed from this world without sin, so "you have returned the treasure entrusted to you." The written Torah presents a mere set of examples. The oral Torah, by contrast, provides not only the model but also the measure and the meaning. The sequence of names, to which our attention is first attracted, allows the message to be stated with great force, and the climactic statement underlines the power of the oral Torah to define the appropriate response to the death of the child. The polemic is clear and, we find, consistent with that of Hillel.

To exemplify the good death—the death in the midst of Torah-study—we come now to the stories about the death of a sage, with special reference to Eliezer b. Hyrcanus. The death scene responds to lists of omens pertinent to one's condition at death:

Ben Azzai says, "Whoever has a serene mind on account of his learning has a good omen for himself, and who does not have a serene mind on account of his learning has a bad omen for himself.

"Whoever has a serene mind on account of his impulse, has a good omen for himself, but if his mind is distressed because of his impulse, it is a bad sign for him.

"For him with whom the sages are satisfied at the hour of death it is a good sign, and for him with whom sages are not satisfied at the hour of death it is a bad sign.

"For whoever has his face turned upward [at death] it is a good sign, and for whoever has his face turned toward the bed it is a bad sign.

"If one is looking at people, it is a good sign, at the wall, a bad sign.

"If one's face is glistening, it is a good sign, glowering, a bad one."

— *The Fathers according to Rabbi Nathan* XXV:I.1

[Ben Azzai] would say, "If one dies in a serene mind, it is a good omen from him, in derangement, it is a bad omen.

". . . while speaking, it is a good omen, in silence, a bad omen.

". . . in repeating words of the Torah, it is a good omen for him, in the midst of discussing business, it is a bad omen.

". . . while doing a religious duty, it is a good omen, while involved with a trivial matter, it is a bad omen.

". . . while happy, it is a good omen, while sad, a bad omen.

". . . while laughing, a good omen, while weeping, a bad omen.

". . . on the eve of the Sabbath, a good omen, at the end of the Sabbath, a bad omen.

". . . on the eve of the Day of Atonement a bad omen, at the end of the Day of Atonement a good omen."

— *The Fathers according to Rabbi Nathan* XXV:III.1

We now have a story illustrating how a great sage dies:

When R. Eliezer was dying—they say it was the eve of the Sabbath [toward dusk]—R. Aqiba and his colleagues came in to see him, and he was dozing in the room, sitting back on a canopied couch. They took seats in the waiting room. Hyrcanus his son came in to remove his phylacteries [which are worn on weekdays but not on the Sabbath, about to begin]. But he did not let him do so, and he was weeping.

Hyrcanus went out and said to the sages, "My lords, it appears to me that my father is deranged."

[Eliezer] said to him, "My son, I am not the one who is deranged, but you are the one who is deranged. For you have neglected to light the lamp for the Sabbath, on which account you may become liable to death penalty inflicted by heaven, but busied yourself with the matter of the phylacteries, on account of which liability is incurred, at worst, merely on the matter of violating the rules of Sabbath rest."

Since sages saw that he was in full command of his faculties, they came in and took up seats before him, but at a distance of four cubits [as was required, because Eliezer was in a state of ostracism on account of his rejection of the decision of the majority in a disputed case]. [Bringing up the case subject to dispute, so to determine whether he had finally accepted the decision of the majority,] they said to him, "My lord, as to a round cushion, a ball, [a shoe when placed on] a shoe maker's last, an amulet, and phylacteries that have been torn, what is the law as to their being susceptible to uncleanness? [Are they regarded as completed and useful objects, therefore susceptible, or as useless or incomplete and therefore not susceptible?]"

[Maintaining his earlier position,] he said to them, "They remain susceptible to uncleanness, and should they become unclean, immerse them as is [without undoing them, e.g., exposing their contents to the water], and take great pains in these matters, for these represent important laws that were stated to Moses at Sinai."

They persisted in addressing to him questions concerning matters of insusceptibility and susceptibility to uncleanness as well as concerning immersion-pools, saying to him, "My lord, what is the rule on this matter?"

He would say to them, "Clean."

And so he went, giving the answer of susceptible to uncleanness to an object that could become unclean, and insusceptible to one that could not become unclean.

The mark of the sage is that, at the hour of death, he continues to engage in study of the Torah. The blessing that the sage receives is that he is able to do so even to his last breath.

After a while R. Eliezer said to sages, "I am amazed at the disciples of the generation, perhaps they may be liable to the death penalty at the hand of Heaven."

They said to him, "My lord, on what account?"

He said to them, "Because you never came and performed the work of apprenticeship to me."

Then he said to Aqiba b. Joseph, "Aqiba, on what account did you not come before me and serve as apprentice to me?"

He said to him, "My lord, I had no time."

He said to him, "I shall be surprised for you if you die a natural death."

And some say, He said nothing to him, but when R. Eliezer spoke as he did to his disciples, forthwith [Aqiba's] heart melted within him.

Said to him R. Aqiba, "My lord, how will I die?"

He said to him, "Aqiba, yours will be the worst."

R. Aqiba entered and took a seat before him and said to him, "My lord, now repeat traditions for me."

He opened a subject and repeated for him three hundred rules concerning the bright spot [to which Lev. 13:1 ff. refers in connection with the skin ailment translated as leprosy].

Then R. Eliezer raised his two arms and folded them on his breast and said, "Woe is me for these two arms, which are like two scrolls of Torahs, which now are departing from the world.

"For were all the oceans ink, all the reeds quills, all men scribes, they could not write down what I have learned in Scripture and repeated in Mishnah-traditions, and derived as lessons from my apprenticeship to sages in the session.

"Yet I have taken away from my masters only as much as does a person who dips his finger into the ocean, and I have taken away for my disciples only so much as a paintbrush takes from a paint tube.

"And furthermore, I can repeat three hundred laws on the rule: *'You shall not permit a sorceress to live.'*"

Some say, "Three thousand."

"But no one ever asked me anything about it, except for Aqiba b. Joseph.

"For one time he said to me, 'My lord, teach me how people plant cucumbers and how they pull them up.'

"I said something and the entire field was filled with cucumbers.

"He said to me, 'My lord, you have taught me how they are planted. Teach me how they are pulled up.'

"I said something, and all of the cucumbers assembled in a single place."

Said R. Eleazar b. Azariah to him, "My lord, as to a shoe that is on the shoemaker's last, what is the law? [Is it susceptible to uncleanness, as a useful object, or insusceptible, since it is not fully manufactured and so finished as a useful object?]"

He said to him, "It is insusceptible to uncleanness."

And so he continued giving answers to questions, ruling of an object susceptible to uncleanness that it is susceptible, and of one insusceptible to uncleanness that it is permanently clean, until his soul went forth as he said the word, "Clean."

Then R. Eleazar b. Azariah tore his clothes and wept, going forth and announcing to sages, "My lords, come and see R. Eliezer, for he is not in a state of purity as to the world to come, since his soul went forth with the word pure on his lips."

After the Sabbath R. Aqiba came and found [Eliezer's corpse being conveyed for burial] on the road from Caesarea to Lud. Then he tore his clothes and ripped his hair, and his blood flowed, and he fell to the earth, crying out and weeping, saying, "Woe is me for you, my lord, woe is me, my master, for you have left the entire generation orphaned."

At the row of mourners he commenced [the lament,] saying, "'My father, my father, chariot of Israel and its horsemen!' I have coins but no expert money-changer to sort them out."

— *The Fathers according to Rabbi Nathan* XXV:IV.1–5

The story serves as a good illustration for three of the positive omens Ben Azzai has listed: while speaking, while repeating words of the Torah, and on the eve of the Sabbath. But he clearly is not represented as happy or cheerful or laughing, so, in the aggregate, I think that an illustration of the omens of Ben Azzai formed a negligible consideration in the minds of the storytellers. The center of interest of the story is Eliezer's complaint against the disciples, who did not study Torah through service to him. But for our purposes, the point is other. It is to underscore that, to the very end, the sage engages in Torah-study and its issues—as though death were not present at all.

It goes without saying, then, that the angel of death holds off while we study the Torah, but takes us—if we are lucky, with a kiss—when we conclude our labor:

R. Seorim, brother of Raba, was sitting before Raba at his deathbed, and saw him falling into a coma. Raba said to him, "Tell [the angel of death] not to torment me as I die."

He said to him, "But aren't you his good buddy?"

He said to him, "Since my star has been handed over into his control, he doesn't pay any attention to me any more."

He said to him, "Show yourself to me in a dream." [Raba] did so.

He asked him, "Did you suffer when you were dying?"

He said to him, "No more than the prick of the leech."

Raba was sitting before R. Nahman at his deathbed, and saw him falling into a coma. He said to him, "Tell [the angel of death] not to torment me as I die."

He said to him, "But aren't you an eminent authority?"

He said to him, "So who is eminent, who is regarded, who is treated as distinguished [by the angel of death]?"

He said to him, "Show yourself to me in a dream." He did so.

He asked him, "Did you suffer when you were dying?"

He said to him, "No more than taking a piece of hair out of the milk, and, I have to tell you, if the Holy One, blessed be he, said to me, 'Now go back to that world as you were before,' I wouldn't do it, for the fear of death is too much to take."

The angel of death made his appearance to R. Sheshet in the market place. He said to him, "Are you going to take me in the market place like a dumb cow? Come to me at my home!"

The angel of death made his appearance to R. Ashi in the market place. He said to him, "Give me thirty days' more so I can review my learning, since you say up there, 'Happy is he who comes up here bringing his learning all ready at hand.'"

So he came along thirty days later. He said to him, "So what's the rush?"

He said to him, "R. Huna bar Nathan is on your heels, and 'no regime may impinge upon its fellow, even by so much as a hair's breadth.'"

The angel of death could not overcome R. Hisda, because his mouth never ceased to recite his learning. He went out and sat on a cedar tree by the house of study. The branch of the cedar cracked, R. Hisda stopped, and the other overcame him.

The angel of death could not get near R. Hiyya. One day he appeared to him in the form of a poor beggar. He came and knocked on the door, saying, "Bring out some food for me." Others brought it out to him.

He said to R. Hiyya, "Aren't you, my lord, going to treat with mercy this man who is standing outside?"

He opened the door to him, and he showed him a fiery rod and made him give up his soul.

—Babylonian Talmud Tractate Moed Qatan 28a

The intersection of the themes of Torah-study, the immortality of the soul, the humility of sages about all matters except for the Torah, and the sagacity of the sage all show us how, once more, the system says the same thing about everything. The upshot for our inquiry is, Torah-study is the path to eternal life, and in this Judaic system portrayed by the classics, that hardly presents a surprise.

WHAT HAPPENS AFTER DEATH

When we die, we go for judgment for our conduct in this life. And that fact brings us to the other aspect of the good death as well as the Torah's picture of what happens then—the good death as the statement of acceptance, submission to God's will, and humility in the face of divine judgment and justice. For we shall now see how the great sage died in an attitude of uncertainty and humility, not taking for granted that through a life of study and practice of the teachings of the Torah, he has forced his way into the Garden of Eden. Rather, the great sage dies in an attitude of humility and awareness of sin. Here we see, moreover, the theory of what happens after death. A broad range of opinions makes its way in the written and oral parts of the Torah, but three points emerge as authoritative: (1) we are judged; (2) we are rewarded or penalized for our life on earth by being sent to either the Garden of Eden or Gehenna; and (3) when the Messiah comes, we will all be raised from the dead. Individual judgment takes place upon death; the resurrection of the dead forms part of the end of time inaugurated by the coming of the Messiah. Here is the classic account of how sages view that matter and of what is at stake in it:

> When R. Yohanan b. Zakkai fell ill, his disciples came in to pay a call on him. When he saw them, he began to cry. His disciples said to him, "Light of Israel! Pillar at the right hand! Mighty hammer! On what account are you crying?"
>
> He said to them, "If I were going to be brought before a mortal king, who is here today and tomorrow gone to the grave, who, should he be angry with me, will not be angry forever, and, if he should imprison me, will not imprison me forever, and if he should put me to death, whose sentence of death is not for eternity, and whom I can appease with the right words or bribe with money, even so, I should weep.
>
> "But now that I am being brought before the King of kings of kings, the Holy One, blessed be he, who endures forever and ever, who, should he be angry with me, will be angry forever, and if he should imprison me, will imprison me forever, and if he should put me to death, whose sentence of death is for eternity, and whom I cannot appease with the right words or bribe with money,
>
> "and not only so, but before me are two paths, one to the Garden of Eden and the other to Gehenna, and I do not know by which path I shall be brought,
>
> "and should I not weep?"
>
> They said to him, "Our master, bless us."
>
> He said to them, "May it be God's will that the fear of Heaven be upon you as much as the fear of mortal man."
>
> His disciples said, "Just so much?"
>
> He said to them, "Would that it were that much. You should know that, when a person commits a transgression, he says, 'I hope no man sees me.'"
>
> When he was dying, he said to them, "Clear out utensils from

the house, because of the uncleanness [of the corpse, which I am about to impart when I die], and prepare a throne for Hezekiah king of Judah, who is coming."

After a life of Torah-study, deeds of compassion, and love of God, Yohanan still trembles at the judgment he faces, for the Torah teaches never to be certain of oneself until death, but to live a life of repentance and prayer. Yohanan does not claim to know whether he will go to the Garden of Eden or to Gehenna. But that is typical of someone who asks no more than that his disciples fear God as much as they fear man—that is, someone with a solid grasp of ordinary reality.

Various sayings and stories in the oral Torah clarify sages' view of the fate of the soul after death. Souls retain consciousness and can even communicate with the living.

R. Hiyya and R. Jonathan were discoursing while walking in a cemetery. The blue fringes [of the show-fringes] of R. Jonathan were trailing on the ground. Said R. Hiyya to him, "Lift them up, so that [the dead] should not say, 'Tomorrow they are coming to us, and now they are ridiculing us.'"

He said to him, "Do the dead know so much as that? And lo, it is written, 'But the dead do not know a thing' (Qoh. 9:5)."

He said to him, "If you have studied Scripture, you have not reviewed what you learned, and if you reviewed what you learned, you failed to do it a third time, and if you did it a third time, then people did not explain the meaning to you.

"'For the living know that they shall die' (Qoh. 9:5) refers to the righteous, for, when they have died, they still are called the living.

"'But the dead know nothing': This refers to the wicked, who, even while they are alive, are called dead, as it is said, 'And you, wicked one, who are slain, the prince of Israel' (Ezek. 21:30)."

—Babylonian Talmud Tractate Berakhot 18A-B

The righteous, when they die, continue to know what happens in the world, but the wicked perish and lose all consciousness. Communication with the dead takes place so that, under certain circumstances, the living may call up the dead and address questions to them:

The father of Samuel held some money for an estate. When he died, Samuel was not with him [so he did not know where the money was]. People called him, "The son of someone who robs estates."

Samuel came after [his father] to the cemetery. He said to them, "I want father."

They said to him, "There are lots of fathers here."

He said to them, "I want Father, son of Father."

They said to him, "There are lots of fathers, sons of fathers, here too."

He said to them, "I want Father, son of Father, the father of Samuel. Where is he?"

They said to him, "He has gone up to the academy in the firmament."

In the meantime he saw Levi, who was seated outside [away from the rest of the deceased].

He said to him, "Why are you seated outside? Why did you not go up?"

He said to him, "They told me that for as many years as you did not go up to the session of R. Efes and so you injured his feelings, we are not going to take you up to the academy in the firmament."

Meanwhile the father [of Samuel] came along. [Samuel] saw that he was both weeping and smiling. He said, "Why are you weeping?"

He said to him, "Because soon you are coming here."

"Why are you smiling?"

"Because you are highly regarded in this world."

He said to him, "If I am highly regarded, then let them take up Levi." So they took Levi up.

He said to him, "As to the money belonging to the estate, where is it?"

He said to him, "Go and take it out of the case of the mill-stones. The money at the top and bottom belongs to us, and what is in the middle belongs to the estate."

He said to him, "Why did you do it that way?"

He said to him, "If thieves come, they will steal ours. If the earth rots the money, it will rot ours."

This story again proves that the deceased know what is going on.

But perhaps the case of Samuel is different, since he is highly regarded.

Since that was the case, [in heaven] they went ahead and announced, "Make room for him."

—Babylonian Talmud Tractate Berakhot 18B

The upshot is straightforward: death brings to the end the life in this world and opens up the life in the world to come, "This world is like a corridor before the world to come" (tractate Abot 4:16), and the world to come is the world that is wholly good. But to understand the Judaic doctrine of death as set forth in the classical documents, we must introduce one further consideration, and that is the coming resurrection of the dead at the end of days. That view is stated in so many words in the following:

R. Jacob says, "You have not got a single religious duty that is written in the Torah, the reward of which is not specified alongside, that does not depend for its fulfillment on the resurrection of the dead. For example, with reference to honor of father and mother, it is written, 'That your days may be prolonged and that it may go well with you' (Deut. 5:16); with regard to sending forth the dam out of the nest: 'That it may be well with you and that you may prolong your days' (Deut. 22:6). Now, if someone's father said to him, 'Climb up into the loft and bring me the pigeons,' and he went up to the loft, sent away the dam and took the young, and climbing down, fell and was killed—what are we to make of this one's 'happiness' and 'length of days'? But the language, 'in order that it may be well with you' refers to a day that is wholly good; and 'in order that your days may be long' means, on the day that is entirely long."

—Babylonian Talmud Tractate Qiddushin 39b

Scripture itself, as our sages read it, refers us toward the coming world of resurrection and eternal life, to which we now turn.

RESURRECTION, REINCARNATION

The belief in the resurrection of the dead to eternal life is joined to the conviction that the Israel of which the Torah speaks, the supernatural community called into being to the covenant of the Torah, forms the focus of the cosmic drama. Israel, for the purposes of resurrection, is defined in strictly theological terms: those who belong to the sacred community and have not separated themselves from it by espousing false doctrine. Such false doctrine involves only a few, but critical matters, beginning with the denial that the Torah promises the resurrection of the dead and that the Torah comes from God. That is to say, those who deny resurrection, which the Torah reveals, do not rise from the dead, a fitting penalty for their sin of arrogant denial of the Torah and its teaching:

All Israelites have a share in the world to come,
    as it is said, "your people also shall be all righteous, they shall inherit the land forever; the branch of my planting, the work of my hands, that I may be glorified" (Is. 60:21).
    And these are the ones who have no portion in the world to come:

He who says, the resurrection of the dead is a teaching which does not derive from the Torah, and the Torah does not come from Heaven; and an Epicurean.

—Mishnah-tractate Sanhedrin 11:1

The Talmud's commentary makes explicit our surmises: "Such a one denied the resurrection of the dead, therefore he will not have a portion in the resurrection of the dead. For all the measures [meted out by] the Holy One, blessed be he, are in accord with the principle of measure for measure."

For sages, the issue was not that the dead would be raised, but that the Torah proved that the dead would be raised. In the following story, minim, that is, heretic Jews, wished to deny that claim and to demonstrate that the Torah contained no such teaching:

Minim asked Rabban Gamaliel, "How do we know that the Holy One, blessed be he, will resurrect the dead?"

He said to them, "It is proved from the Torah, from the Prophets, and from the Writings." But they did not accept his proofs.

"From the Torah: for it is written, 'And the Lord said to Moses, Behold, you shall sleep with your fathers and rise up' (Deut. 31:16)."

They said to him, "But perhaps the sense of the passage is, 'And the people will rise up' (Deut. 31:16)?"

"From the Prophets: as it is written, 'Thy dead men shall live, together with my dead body they shall arise. Awake and sing, you that live in the dust, for your dew is as the dew of herbs, and the earth shall cast out its dead' (Is. 26:19)."

"But perhaps that refers to the dead whom Ezekiel raised up."

"From the Writings, as it is written, 'And the roof of your mouth, like the best wine of my beloved, that goes down sweetly, causing the lips of those who are asleep to speak' (Song 7:9)."

"But perhaps this means that the dead will move their lips?"

[The minim would not concur in Gamaliel's view] until he cited for them the following verse: "'Which the Lord swore to your fathers to give to them' (Deut. 11:21)—to them and not to you, so proving from the Torah that the dead will live."

And there are those who say that it was the following verse that he cited to them: "'But you who cleaved to the Lord your God are alive, everyone of you this day' (Deut. 4:4). Just as on this day all of you are alive, so in the world to come all of you will live."

—Babylonian Talmud Tractate Sanhedrin 90a

At the same time, sages had to take up the challenge of reasonable Gentiles, who found the belief implausible. For them, questions of rational proof, not demonstrations of truth based on the Torah, had to be devised, and in the following stories we see how appeal to nature, not to revelation, was set forth:

Queen Cleopatra asked R. Meir, saying, "I know that the dead will live, for it is written, 'And [the righteous] shall blossom forth out of your city like the grass of the earth' (Ps. 72:16).

"But when they rise, will they rise naked or in their clothing?"

He said to her, "It is an argument a fortiori based on the grain of wheat.

"Now if a grain of wheat, which is buried naked, comes forth in many garments, the righteous, who are buried in their garments, all the more so [will rise in many garments]!"

Caesar said to Rabban Gamaliel, "You maintain that the dead will live. But they are dust, and can the dust live?"

His daughter said to him, "Allow me to answer him:

"There are two potters in our town, one who works with water, the other who works with clay. Which is the more impressive?"

He said to her, "The one who works with water."

She said to him, "If he works with water, will he not create even
more out of clay?"

A Tannaite authority of the house of R. Ishmael [taught],
"[Resurrection] is a matter of an argument a fortiori based on the
case of a glass utensil.

"Now if glassware, which is the work of the breath of a mortal
man, when broken, can be repaired,

"A mortal man, who is made by the breath of the Holy One,
blessed be he, how much the more so [that he can be repaired, in
the resurrection of the dead]."

A min said to R. Ammi, "You say that the dead will live. But
they are dust, and will the dust live?"

He said to him, "I shall draw a parable for you. To what may
the matter be compared?

"It may be compared to the case of a mortal king, who said to
his staff, 'Go and build a great palace for me, in a place in which
there is no water or dirt [for bricks].'

"They went and built it, but after a while it collapsed.

"He said to them, 'Go and rebuild it in a place in which there
are dirt and water [for bricks].'

"They said to him, 'We cannot do so.'

"He became angry with them and said to them, 'In a place in
which there is neither water nor dirt you were able to build, and
now in a place in which there are water and dirt, how much the
more so [should you be able to build it]!'

"And if you [the min] do not believe it, go to a valley and look
at a rat, which today is half-flesh and half-dirt and tomorrow will
turn into a creeping thing, made all of flesh. Will you say that it
takes much time? Then go up to a mountain and see that today
there is only one snail, but tomorrow it will rain and the whole of
it will be filled with snails."

—Babylonian Talmud Tractate Sanhedrin 90b–91a

The resurrection of the dead forms a principal component of the Judaic theology of death and the afterlife. It comes to critical expression, moreover, in the liturgy of the synagogue. The prayers of petition, recited three times a day, include at the head the following blessing: "Your might, O Lord, is boundless. Your loving kindness sustains the living, your great mercies give life to the dead. You support the falling, heal the ailing, free the fettered. You keep your faith with those that sleep in the dust. Whose power can compare with yours? You are the master of life and death and deliverance. Faithful are you in giving life to the dead. Praised are you, Lord, master of life and death."[3]

The logic of the Judaic view proves blatant here: master of life also is lord over death, and who gives life once can and will bestow life a second time. Death too will die, and that view is stated in so many words:

> Ulla contrasted [these two verses]: "It is written, 'He will destroy death forever and the Lord God will wipe away tears from all faces' (Is. 25:9), and it is written, 'For the child shall die a hundred years old . . . there shall no more thence an infant of days' (Is. 65:20).
>
> "There is no contradiction. The one speaks of Israel, the other of idolators."
>
> But what do idolators want there [in the reestablished state after the resurrection]?
>
> It is to those concerning whom it is written, "And strangers shall stand and feed your flocks, and the sons of the alien shall be your plowmen and your vine dressers" (Is. 61:5).
>
> —Babylonian Talmud Tractate Sanhedrin 90b–91a

Resurrection represents God's victory over death, the final act of creation. And that act takes place with the coming of the Messiah. No account of the Judaic view of the afterlife can omit reference to the messianic question: When, why, and for what purpose will the Messiah come?

The Messiah will come to Israel when Israel freely gives what God passionately desires but cannot coerce, which is Israel's love for God expressed through Israel's humble acceptance of the Torah. It is Israel's history that works out and expresses Israel's relationship with God. The principal result of Israel's loyal adherence to the Torah and its religious duties will be Israel's humble acceptance of God's rule. The humility, under all conditions, makes God love Israel.

> "It was not because you were greater than any people that the Lord set his love upon you and chose you" [Deut. 7:7]. The Holy One, blessed be he, said to Israel, "I love you because even when I bestow greatness upon you, you humble yourselves before me. I bestowed greatness upon Abraham, yet he said to me, 'I am but dust and ashes' [Gen. 18:27]; upon Moses and Aaron, yet they said, 'But I am a worm and no man' [Ps. 22:7]. But with the heathens it is not so. I bestowed greatness upon Nimrod, and he said, 'Come, let us build us a city' [Gen. 11:4]; upon Pharaoh, and he said, 'Who are they among all the gods of the countries?' [2 Kings 18:35]; upon Nebuchadnezzar, and he said, 'I will ascend above the heights of the clouds' [Isa. 14:14]; upon Hiram, king of Tyre, and he said, 'I sit in the seat of God, in the heart of the seas' [Ezek. 28:2]."
> —Babylonian Talmud Tractate Hullin 89a

The system emerges complete, each of its parts stating precisely the same message as is revealed in the whole. The issue of the Messiah and the meaning of Israel's history framed through the Messiah myth convey in their terms precisely the same position that we find everywhere else in all other symbolic components of the rabbinic system and canon. The heart of the matter is Israel's subservience to God's will, as expressed in the Torah and embodied in the teachings and lives of the great sages. When Israel fully accepts God's rule, the Messiah will come. Until Israel subjects itself to God's rule, the Jews will be subjugated to pagan domination. Since the condition of Israel governs, Israel itself holds the key to its own redemption. But it can achieve this only by throwing away the key!

The paradox must be crystal clear: Israel acts to redeem itself through the opposite of self-determination, namely, subjugating itself to God. Israel's power lies in its negation of power. Its destiny lies in giving up all pretense at deciding its own destiny. Weakness is the ultimate strength; forbearance, the final act of self-assertion; passive resignation, the sure step toward liberation. (The parallel is the crucified Christ.) Israel's freedom is engraved on the tablets of the commandments of God: to be free is freely to obey. That is not the meaning associated with these words in the minds of others who, like the sages of the rabbinical canon, declared their view of what Israel must do to secure the coming of the Messiah.

The passage, praising Israel for its humility, completes the circle begun with the description of Bar Kokhba as arrogant and boastful. Gentile kings are boastful; Israelite kings are humble. In all, the Messiah myth deals with a very concrete and limited consideration of the national life and character. The theory of Israel's history and destiny as it was expressed within that myth interprets matters in terms of a single criterion. What others within the Israelite world had done or in the future would do with the conviction that, at the end of time, God would send a (or the) Messiah to "save" Israel; it was a single idea for the sages of the Mishnah and the Talmuds and collections of scriptural exegesis. And that conception stands at the center of their system; it shapes and is shaped by their system. In context, the Messiah expresses the system's meaning and so makes it work.

Sages maintained that keeping the law now signified keeping the faith: the act of hope. This means that the issues of the law were drawn upward into the highest realm of Israelite consciousness. Keeping the law in the right way is represented as not merely right or expedient. It is the way to bring the Messiah, the son of David. This is stated by Levi, as follows:

> Said R. Levi, "If Israel would keep a single Sabbath in the proper way, forthwith the son of David would come.
>
> "What is the Scriptural basis for this view? Moses said, 'Eat it today, for today is a Sabbath to the Lord; today you will not find it in the field' (Ex. 16:25)."
>
> And it says, "For thus said the Lord God, the Holy One of Israel, 'In returning and rest you shall be saved; in quietness and in trust shall be your strength. And you would not' (Is. 30:15)."
>
> —Yerushalmi Taanit 1:1.IX

Rabbis insisted the Messiah would come in a process extending over a long period of time, thus not imposing a caesura upon the existence of the nation and disrupting its ordinary life. Accordingly, the messianic hope was something gradual, to be worked toward, not a sudden cataclysmic event. That conception was fully in accord with the notion that the everyday deeds of people formed a pattern continuous with the salvific history of Israel, that is, the individual Israelite from death, and the holy people from the thrall of the idolators:

> One time R. Hiyya the Elder and R. Simeon b. Halapta were walking in the valley of Arabel at daybreak. They saw that the light of the morning star was breaking forth. Said R. Hiyya the Elder to R. Simeon b. Halapta, "Son of my master, this is what the redemption of Israel is like—at first, little by little, but in the end it will go along and burst into light.
>
> "What is the Scriptural basis for this view? 'Rejoice not over me, O my enemy; when I fall, I shall rise; when I sit in darkness, the Lord will be a light to me' (Mic. 7:8).
>
> "So, in the beginning, 'When the virgins were gathered to-

gether the second time, Mordecai was sitting at the king's gate'
(Est. 2:19).

"But afterward: 'So Haman took the robes and the horse, and
he arrayed Mordecai and made him ride through the open square
of the city, proclaiming, Thus shall it be done to the man whom
the king delights to honor' (Est. 6:11).

"And in the end: 'Then Mordecai went out from the presence
of the king in royal robes of blue and white, with a great golden
crown and a mantle of fine linen and purple, while the city of Susa
shouted and rejoiced' (Est. 8:15).

"And finally: 'The Jews had light and gladness and joy and
honor' (Est. 8:16)."

—Palestinian Talmud Tractate Yoma 3:2

The emphasis upon the slow but steady advent of the Messiah's
day is entirely consonant with the notion that the Messiah will
come when Israel's condition warrants it. The improvement in
standards of observing the Torah, therefore, to be effected by
the nation's obedience to the sages will serve as a guidepost on
the road to redemption. The moral condition of the nation ultimately guarantees salvation. God will respond to Israel's regeneration, planning all the while to save the saved, that is, those
who save themselves.

The hope for the Messiah's coming is further joined to the
moral condition of each individual Israelite. That once more
underscores the tight connection between sin, arrogance, and
death, and atonement, reconciliation, the coming of the Messiah, and resurrection. Hence the messianic fulfillment was
made to depend on the repentance of Israel. The coming of the
Messiah depended not on historical action but on moral regeneration. From a force that moved Israelites to take up weapons
on the battlefield, the messianic hope and yearning were transformed into motives for spiritual regeneration and ethical be-

havior. The energies released in the messianic fervor were then linked to rabbinical government, through which Israel would form the godly society. When we reflect that the message, "If you want it, He too wants it to be," comes in a generation confronting a dreadful disappointment, its full weight and meaning become clear.

Israel's salvation depends wholly upon Israel itself. Two things follow. First, the Jews were made to take up the burden of guilt for their own sorry situation. But, second, they gained not only responsibility for, but also power over, their fate. They could do something about salvation, just as their sins had brought about their tragedy. This message promised strength to the weak and hope to the despairing. No one could be asked to believe that the Messiah would come very soon. The events of the day testified otherwise. The counsel of the Talmud's sages was patience and consequential deeds. People could not hasten things, but they could do something. The duty of Israel, in the meantime, was to accept the sovereignty of heavenly government. We conclude with where we began: how sages confronted death:

> R. Abbahu was bereaved. One of his children had passed away from him. R. Jonah and R. Yosé went up [to comfort him]. When they called on him, out of reverence for him, they did not express to him a word of Torah. He said to them, "May the rabbis express a word of Torah."
>
> They said to him, "Let our master teach us."
>
> He said to them, "Now if on regard to the government below, in which there is no reliability, [but only] lying, deceit, favoritism, and bribe taking—
>
> "which is here today and gone tomorrow—
>
> "if concerning that government, it is said, And the relatives of the felon come and inquire after the welfare of the judges and of

the witnesses, as if to say, 'We have nothing against you, for you judged honestly' [M. San. 6:9],

"on regard to the government above, in which there is reliability, but no lying, deceit, favoritism, or bribe taking—

"and which endures forever and to all eternity—

"all the more so are we obligated to accept upon ourselves the just decree [of that heavenly government]."

And it says, "That the Lord . . . may show you mercy, and have compassion on you . . . " (Deut. 13:17).

—Yerushalmi Sanhedrin 6:9.III

It follows that salvation for Israel depended upon adherence to the Torah and acceptance of its discipline. God's will in heaven and the sage's words of Torah-teaching on earth constituted Torah. And Israel would be saved through Torah, so the sage was the savior—especially the humble one. The humblest of them all would be the sage-Messiah, victor over time and circumstance, Savior of Israel, the One who would bring victory over death.

The appearance of a messianic eschatology encompassing the resurrection of the dead fully consonant with the larger characteristic of the rabbinic system—with its stress on the viewpoints and proof-texts of Scripture, its interest in what was happening to Israel, its focus upon the national-historical dimension of the life of the group—joins issues of individual life and death to those affecting God's relationship with humanity through holy Israel. If people wanted to reach the end of time, in history, and to overcome death, in the private life, they had to rise above time, that is, history, and stand off at the side of great movements of political and military character. Israel must turn away from time and change, submit to whatever happens, so as to win for itself the only government worth having, that is, God's rule, accomplished through God's anointed agent, the Messiah.

R. Joshua b. Levi found Elijah standing at the door of the burial vault of R. Simeon b. Yohai. He said to him, "Am I going to come to the world to come?"

He said to him, "If this master wants."

Said R. Joshua b. Levi, "Two did I see, but a third voice did I hear."

He said to him, "When is the Messiah coming?"

He said to him, "Go and ask him."

"And where is he sitting?"

"At the gate of the city."

"And what are the marks that indicate who he is?"

"He is sitting among the poor who suffer illness, and all of them untie and tie their bandages all together, but he unties them and ties them one by one. He is thinking, 'Perhaps I may be wanted, and I do not want to be held up.'"

He went to him, saying to him, "Peace be unto you, my master and teacher."

He said to him, "Peace be unto you, son of Levi."

He said to him, "When is the master coming?"

He said to him, "Today."

He went back to Elijah, who said to him, "What did he tell you?"

He said to him, "'Peace be unto you, son of Levi.'"

He said to him, "He [thereby] promised you and your father the world to come."

He said to him, "But he lied to me. For he said to me, 'I am coming today,' but he did not come."

He said to him, "This is what he said to you, 'Today, if you will obey his voice' (Ps. 95:7)."

—Babylonian Talmud Tractate Sanhedrin 93b

CHAPTER 3

Islam

JONATHAN E. BROCKOPP

WAYS OF DYING AND THE GOOD DEATH

The end of life on earth, according to Islam, is the end of a period of testing and trial. God will gather all peoples to him on the last day to judge them according to their earthly deeds, and they will then proceed either to hell or to heaven. How one dies is therefore a matter of some concern to Muslims, since those last days can be a time to reflect on a life of good and evil acts, and perhaps a time to redress some misdeed of the past. As a religion that emphasizes the importance of good actions over a lifetime, however, it is not possible to make up for a life of evil through a deathbed conversion, as the Qur'an explicitly states: "God shall not turn towards those who do evil deeds until, when one of them is visited by death, he says, 'Indeed now I repent!'" (4:22).[1] So while some deaths are better than others, God judges persons on the basis of their whole lives and the fulfillment of their duties both to God (such as prayer and fasting) and to other human beings (such as giving alms and protecting the weak).

The best of deaths, according to Islam, involves dying while devoting one's actions entirely to God. Accordingly, Muslims honor the deaths of martyrs who have given their lives for the faith; Muslims might also take the pilgrimage to Mecca in their old age in hopes of dying in Mecca or on the way. Likewise, death while fighting in a religiously sanctioned war (jihad) results in being admitted directly into heaven. In all these situations, however, one may never seek death; Islam forbids suicide, so placing oneself purposely in danger during jihad, or during the pilgrimage, is absolutely forbidden.

The Islamic martyr tradition is filled with examples of those who have been persecuted for their faith. During the Prophet's lifetime, the early Muslim community was attacked by the surrounding tribes, and many Muslims lost their lives. Sumayyah bt. Kubbat is famous as the first martyr in Islam; her master tried to force her to leave the new faith of Islam, and she died when he stabbed her with a spear. Others were tortured or died for their convictions, and even the life of the Prophet was threatened. Eventually, the early community was able to defend itself in a series of skirmishes in which dozens of Muslims, both men and women, died in battle. The Muslims emerged victorious, however, and the tradition numbers these individuals among its greatest martyrs.

The grandson of the Prophet, Husayn, is also considered a martyr, particularly in the Shiite tradition, where he is known as the Lord of the Martyrs. The month in which he was killed (Muharram) is still marked with processions of mourning throughout the Shiite world. In 1978, just before the revolution in Iran, the Ayatollah Khomeini used imagery from Husayn's martyrdom to call for similar acts of self-sacrifice by the Iranian people:

> With the approach of Muharram, we are about to begin the month of epic heroism and self-sacrifice—the month in which blood triumphed over the sword, the month in which truth condemned falsehood for all eternity and branded the mark of disgrace upon the forehead of all oppressors and satanic governments; the month that has taught successive generations throughout history the path of victory over the bayonet; the month that proves the superpowers may be defeated by the word of truth; the month in which the

leader of the Muslims taught us how to struggle against all the tyrants of history, showed us how the clenched fists of those who seek freedom, desire independence, and proclaim the truth may triumph over tanks, machine guns, and the armies of Satan, how the word of truth may obliterate falsehood.[2]

Martyrdom is valued in Islam because it is a submission of personal desires to the good of the whole. In the case of Husayn, fighting a hopeless battle against the forces of a despotic governor exposed the true nature of that governor. Because of their acts of self-sacrifice, martyrs are understood to have direct access to heaven, to be among God's elect. The famous Muslim mystic al-Hallaj was persecuted for his beliefs, but so strong was his conviction that he would be admitted into God's presence that he is reported to have been singing as he was taken off to the gallows, and these words have been ascribed to him: "*uqtiluni ya asdiqa'i fa-fi qatli hayati*—kill me, O my friends, for in my death is my life!"

In the same way, stories abound of early Muslims throwing themselves into battle with the hope of dying "in God's path." The Prophet is said to have wished for three lives so he could lose each of them in fighting for the faith. Another story from these early battles concerns a soldier taking a break in the midst of fighting and suddenly throwing down his dates, saying: "Am I so eager for the good things of this world that I should sit here and finish these morsels in my hand?" He then grabbed his sword and raced back to the front, eventually losing his life.[3]

With these words, the soldier was repeating a familiar refrain from the Qur'an: the good to be found in this world is mere chance compared to the good things that God has prepared in the world to come. Addressing a group of unbelievers who claimed to be the only ones to be admitted to heaven, the Qur'an says:

Say: "If the final abode with God is yours exclusively, and not for other people, then long for death—if you are among those who speak the truth."

—The Cow 2:94

This is the first part of Islam's attitude toward death: it is to be seen as the passage to life in the hereafter, either heaven or hell. The second point is a corollary: only God controls the span of life and the time of death. To the unbelievers, the Qur'an responds: "Wherever you may be, death will overtake you, though you should be in raised-up towers" (4:80). Not even the rich and powerful can escape death, but there is more. Elsewhere, the Qur'an retorts: "Say, 'God gives you life then makes you die, then He shall gather you to the Day of Resurrection, wherein there is no doubt, but most do not know'" (45:26). In its theology of death, the Qur'an does not merely see God as the cold hand of fate, but as a different kind of active principle in the world, as the Author of life and death. From this general attitude toward death in this world, the Qur'an builds a theology of jihad exemplified in the following two verses:

So let them fight in the way of God who sell the present life for the world to come; and whosoever fights in the way of God and is slain, or conquers, We shall bring him a mighty wage.

—Women 4:76

And those who are slain in the way of God, He will not send their works astray. He will guide them, and dispose their minds aright, and He will admit them to Paradise, that He has made known to them.

—Muhammad 47:4–6

In the first of these verses, the image of the marketplace is used, and believers are urged to risk their lives for the hope of a heavenly reward. As will be discussed below, the marketplace imagery also pervades discussion of Judgment Day, when great scales are set up to weigh one's sins against one's good deeds. The hadith record reinforces this idea of aiming for a heavenly reward. The following statement is attributed to the Caliph ᶜUmar, one of the Prophet's closest companions, and he exchanges the three great qualities of the old Arabian warrior (reputation, noble descent, and chivalry) with three qualities of the Muslim warrior:

> Malik—Yahya b. Saᶜid—ᶜUmar b. al-Khattab said: "The reputation of a believer is his fear of God; his noble descent is his faith; and his chivalry is his religious disposition. Cowardice and courage are natural instincts which God places where He wishes: the coward flees even from his own mother and father, while the courageous fights for that which he cannot bring back in his saddlebags. Dying in battle is just one sort of death, but the true martyr is the one who sacrifices himself in anticipation of God's reward."[4]

ᶜUmar's emphasis on the importance of intention is a key part of the difference between a normal warrior and a Muslim risking his life for God's cause. Further, since the emphasis is on sacrificing oneself for the greater good of the Muslims, death in battle is "just one sort of death." In fact, Muslims may speak of fighting in battle as the "lesser jihad"; the greater jihad is fighting against one's own sinful nature. After the revolution of 1979, the Ayatollah Khomeini urged his followers to engage in this greater jihad:

> How much longer do you wish to continue your sleep of neglect, to remain immersed in evil and corruption? Fear God and the consequences of your deeds; wake up from your sleep of neglect. You have not yet awakened and taken the first step on the path of wayfaring, for awakening is the first step. Yes, you are asleep.

Your eyes are open, but your hearts are deep in sleep. If your hearts were not intoxicated with sleep and black and rusted with sin, you would not be able to continue so tranquilly and heedlessly with your wrong deeds and words. Were you to think a little about the hereafter and the places of horror it contains, or to reflect on the heavy duties and responsibilities you bear, you would take these matters more seriously.

You have another world ahead of you; there is resurrection and a return to the divine presence awaiting you. You are not like other creatures who face no return. Why do you not take heed?[5]

Khomeini's words emphasize that Muslims need to devote the same zeal of the martyr to their everyday actions, since all sins will be weighed and judged on the last day. Because dying in battle is "just one sort of death," one must be prepared to face God's judgment at any time.

Like other traditions that forbid suicide, Islam has to draw a clear line between seeking God's reward as a martyr in battle and seeking death. One's aim, whether on the battlefield or in everyday life, must be to submit personal desires to the Divine. Further, since God is the author of life and death, assisted suicide by a person suffering from a fatal illness is usually not allowed. Yet it does not necessarily follow from this distinction that all forms of euthanasia are always wrong, particularly in cases where methods are passive, such as the removal of a machine that is keeping a patient from dying. Suffering is considered part of the imperfection of earthly existence, which must be endured.

Of course, most Muslims die perfectly ordinary deaths, far removed from the battlefield, and despite the hope of eternal life in paradise, death remains a profoundly tragic event for Muslims. In a famous story by the Egyptian novelist Naguib Mahfouz, the death of the family patriarch is described by his son as a devastation, yet the father's hope of eternal reward is expressed through his attempt to die with the words of the Muslim confession on his lips, to die while worshiping God.

> The bottom half of his father's body lay on the bed while the upper half rested on Amina's breast. The man's chest was heaving up and down mechanically as he emitted a strange rattling sound not of this world. His eyes had a new blind look, which suggested that they could not see anything or express the man's internal struggle. . . .
>
> The father moved as if trying to sit up, and the convulsions of his chest increased. He stretched out the forefinger of his right hand and then that of his left. When Amina saw this, her face contracted with pain. She bent down toward his ear and recited in an audible voice, "There is no god but God, and Muhammad is the Messenger of God." She kept repeating these words until his hand became still. Kamal understood that his father, no longer able to speak, had asked Amina to recite the Muslim credo on his behalf and that the inner meaning of this final hour would never be revealed. To describe it as pain, terror, or a swoon would have been a pointless conjecture. At any rate it could not last long, for it was too momentous and significant to be part of ordinary life.[6]

In this novel, Mahfouz draws on imagery from the life of the Prophet himself, who also died quietly in his wife's arms after a short illness. It is at the moment of death that the full tragedy of this world is made clear and that hope for the world to come is strongest. One traditional account of the Prophet's death suggests that he, unlike others, was given knowledge of the time of his death beforehand, so he went to the place where martyrs from an earlier battle were buried in order to address the dead.

> ᶜAbdallah b. ᶜUmar—ᶜUbayd b. Jubayr—ᶜAbdallah b. ᶜAmr b. al-ᶜAs—Abu Muwayhibah, a freedman of the apostle, said: In the

middle of the night the apostle sent for me and told me that he was
ordered to pray for the dead in this cemetery and that I was to go
with him. I went; and when he stood among them he said, "Peace
upon you, O people of the graves! Happy are you that you are so
much better off than men here. Dissensions have come like waves
of darkness one after the other, the last being worse than the first."
Then he turned to me and said, "I have been given the choice between the keys of the treasuries of this world and long life here followed by Paradise, and meeting my Lord and Paradise at once." I
urged him to choose the former, but he said that he had chosen the
latter. Then he prayed for the dead there and went away. Then it
was that the illness through which God took him began.[7]

Like that of Kamal's father, the Prophet's death was a profoundly tragic event for the early community of Muslims, and
some even refused to believe that he had died, including his
longtime friend ʿUmar. In this account, another companion of
the Prophet, Abu Bakr, addresses ʿUmar and the crowd of believers by citing a verse from the Qur'an.

Al-Zuhri and Saʿid b. al-Musayyid—Abu Hurayrah: When the
apostle was dead ʿUmar got up and said: "Some of the disaffected
will allege that the apostle is dead, but by God he is not dead: he
has gone to his Lord as Moses b. ʿImran went and was hidden
from his people for forty days, returning to them after it was said
that he had died. By God, the apostle will return as Moses returned and will cut off the hands and feet of men who allege that
the apostle is dead." When Abu Bakr heard what was happening
he came to the door of the mosque as ʿUmar was speaking to the
people. He paid no attention but went in to ʿAʾisha's house to the
apostle, who was lying covered by a mantle of Yamani cloth. He
went and uncovered his face and kissed him, saying, "You are
dearer than my father and mother. You have tasted the death

which God had decreed: a second death will never overtake you."
Then he replaced the mantle on the apostle's face and went out.
ᶜUmar was still speaking and he said, "Gently, ᶜUmar, be quiet."
But ᶜUmar refused and went on talking, and when Abu Bakr saw
that he would not be silent he went forward to the people who,
when they heard his words, came to him and left ᶜUmar. Giving
thanks and praise to God he said: "O men, if anyone worships
Muhammad, Muhammad is dead: if anyone worships God, God
is alive, immortal." Then he recited this verse: "Muhammad is
nothing but an apostle. Apostles have passed away before him.
Can it be that if he were to die or be killed you would turn back on
your heels? He who turns back does no harm to God and God will
reward the grateful." (3:138)[8]

Abu Bakr's clear words remind the Muslim that even the
Prophet, God's chosen apostle, still had to face death at God's
decree. Like most Muslims, the Prophet did not die engaged in
a specific act of worship, such as the pilgrimage or the jihad, nor
did he die as a martyr like his grandson Husayn. Rather, the
Prophet devoted all his actions to the worship of God, and in so
doing provides the best example of how a Muslim should die.

WHAT HAPPENS AFTERWARD—HEAVEN AND HELL

When a Muslim dies, the body is washed and carried to the
grave to be buried. Those who remain behind grieve for a long
period of mourning, but what happens to the body and soul of
the believer? The Qur'an teaches that body and soul will be
united at a day of resurrection, an act that is described as easy
for the Author of life and death. This message is found in many
places throughout the Qur'an, but the version from the sura Ya
Sin is the one often recited at funerals. After a long list of God's
signs in nature—bringing forth grain from seed, determining
the times of sun and moon, and so forth—the Qur'an addresses
the unbelievers:

And the Trumpet shall be blown; then behold, they are sliding
down from their tombs unto their Lord.

They say, "Alas for us! Who roused us out of our sleeping
place? This is what the All-merciful promised, and the Envoys
spoke truly."

It was only one Cry; then behold, they are all arraigned before
Us: "So today no soul shall be wronged anything, and you shall not
be recompensed, except according to what you have been doing.

"See the inhabitants of Paradise today are busy in their rejoic-
ing, they and their spouses, reclining upon couches in the shade;
therein they have fruits, and they have all that they call for."
"Peace!"—such is the greeting, from a Lord All-compassionate.

—Ya Sin 36:51–58

As this sura promises, the believers will enter heaven, and the
unbelievers will be condemned to hell. All this will occur at the
end of time, when God will judge everyone. The actual theology of resurrection will be dealt with in the next section; here
our primary interest is in the heaven and hell that the Qur'an
describes. Of the three great monotheistic scriptures, none is
more explicit than the Qur'an in detailing the joy and suffering
of the world to come. Just as the above description of heaven re-
calls the pleasure of a shady garden on a warm summer's day, the
most vivid representations of hell in the Qur'an depict sinners
languishing in the desert. Especially in the Meccan suras, when
Muhammad was preaching to a crowd of skeptical polytheists,
vivid depictions of hell abound:

The Companions of the Left (O Companions of the Left!)
mid burning winds and boiling waters
and the shadow of a smoking blaze
neither cool, neither goodly;
and before that they lived in ease,
and persisted in the Great Sin, ever saying,

"What, when we are dead and become dust and bones, shall we
   indeed be raised up?
What, and our fathers, the ancients?"
Say: "The ancients, and the later folk shall be gathered to the
   appointed time of a known day.
Then you erring ones, you that cried lies,
you shall eat of a tree called Zakkoum,
and you shall fill therewith your bellies
and drink on top of that boiling water
lapping it down like thirsty camels."

—The Terror 56:40–55

Here, even the words of the skeptical polytheists are preserved
by the Qur'an as they ask how God will bring back to life the
very bones that can be seen in the desert. The Qur'an calls these
challenges to its message "crying lies" and sees hell as a fitting
end for these people. Other descriptions pick up these same
themes:

Faces on that day humbled,
labouring, toilworn,
roasting at a scorching fire,
watered at a boiling fountain,
no food for them but cactus thorn
unfattening, unappeasing hunger.

—The Enveloper 88:2–7

In these passages, the Qur'an is tailoring its description to the
desert-dwelling Meccans, describing for them a hell of suffering
that mimics and intensifies the pain of life in the Arabian desert.
The burning heat of the desert sun is increased by fire, and the
thirsty receive only boiling water or melted copper to drink.
   Popular preachers in other parts of the Muslim world have

taken Qur'anic imagery of the world to come and expanded upon it. Here is one version from East Africa, referring to the journey taken by believers as they enter paradise:

> There, near the end of their ordeal, they will be allowed to drink from Kawthar, the lake of abundance, which belongs to Muhammad personally and so only his followers and friends may drink from it. Once a soul of a person has drunk a sip, that person will never be thirsty again, and never be ill. The water is sweeter than sugar, whiter than snow and has such a pleasant smell that no one who has ever tasted it will want to go back to earth. The lake Kawthar is so large that it would stretch from Mecca to the Yemen. There is also the *tawba,* that is the tree of remorse, whose fruits are food for every true believer in paradise as often as he wishes. Its branches and rich foliage are so large that they provide pleasant cool shade for all the inhabitants of paradise, sheltering them from the dazzling light that shines down from the Holy Throne above.[9]

Muslims believe that heaven and hell were created along with the earth and are currently in existence. In fact, the Prophet is said to have traveled to heaven during his visionary "night journey" and visited with Moses and other prophets already residing there. Further, there is a famous hadith where the Prophet explains the scorching winds of the Arabian desert as originating in the furnaces of hell. The question arises: How can people be consigned to heaven or hell before the actual Judgment Day? It seems that all souls will arise on that final day, but certain punishments and rewards are actually meted out before bodies and souls are reunited. As noted above, Muhammad addressed the "people of the graves" before his own death, and in the following account, he actually hears the cries of anguish of those suffering punishment in the tomb.

Zayd b. Thabit said: "One day we were in an enclosure belonging
to the tribe of al-Najjar, in the company of the Apostle of God,
who was riding on a mule. Suddenly the beast threatened to throw
him down, by making a side-leap, being terrified by five or six
graves. The Apostle of God asked: Who of you knew the people
who were buried here? A man said: I. The Apostle of God asked:
When did they die? He answered: In the time of polytheism. Then
the Apostle of God said: Verily, this generation is tormented in
their tombs, and were it not that you would object to bury one another, I would pray God to let you hear of the punishment in the
tomb what I hear of it. Then he turned to us, saying: Take refuge
with God from the punishment in the tomb. This he said twice."[10]

Muslim theologians occupied themselves for centuries with the
question of explaining this punishment, and they developed the
following doctrine:

Regarding the Faithful two things are possible; if he has been obe-
dient, he will be exempt from the punishment of the tomb; he will
have to suffer the pressure only. If he has been a sinner, he will
suffer the punishment of the tomb as well as the pressure; but the
punishment will cease on the next Friday and it will not return before the day of resurrection. If he dies on a Friday or in the night
before a Friday, the punishment and the pressure will last one hour
only and the punishment will not return before the day of resurrection. If the dead man be an infidel, his punishment will last till
the day of resurrection, and will be suspended only on Fridays and
during Ramadan.[11]

The doctrine of punishment in the tomb seems to suggest that
the dead do not sleep until the day of judgment in some state of
ultimate unconsciousness; rather, they exist in a type of limbo.
Further, many Muslims believe that some of the dead are aware

of earthly goings-on and able to affect events in this world. Such belief has led to the popular visitation of saints' tombs in much of the Muslim world to receive blessings from these holy men and women. While paradise and hell await all humankind on the day of judgment, a foretaste of that afterlife may be provided in the tomb itself.

RESURRECTION

There is no reincarnation in Islam; each soul has only one chance to "prove its worth." On the day of judgment, the souls of all humankind will be reunited with their bodies; the reunited body and soul will then rise from the dead and await the final judgment of the Creator to see whether they will spend eternity in heaven or in hell. This day is described in the Qur'an as a time of great tribulation on earth. Many Muslims believe that humankind will fall away from belief in God at the end of time, that the Qur'an will no longer be studied, that great plagues and earthquakes will signal the coming of the antichrist who will rule the earth for a while. The antichrist will then be defeated by a messiah (sometimes identified with the second coming of Jesus), who will establish a final reign of justice before God calls all souls to return to him. Judgment Day is described in the following terms by the Qur'an:

> The earth altogether shall be His handful on the Day of Resurrection, and the heavens shall be rolled up in His right hand. Glory be to Him! High be He exalted above that they associate!
>
> For the Trumpet shall be blown, and whosoever is in the heavens and whosoever is in the earth shall swoon, save whom God wills. Then it shall be blown again, and lo, they shall stand beholding.
>
> And the earth shall shine with the light of its Lord, and the Book shall be set in place, and the Prophets and witnesses shall be

brought, and justly the issue be decided between them, and they not wronged.

Every soul shall be paid in full for what it has wrought; and He knows very well what they do.

—The Companies 39:67–70

The very idea of bodily resurrection was a difficult one for the early Muslims, and the Qur'an spends much time explaining that God can make dead bones come to life. For instance, the Qur'an records the following views: "They say, 'There is nothing but our present life; we die, and we live, and nothing but Time destroys us—'" To which God responds, "Of that they have no knowledge; they merely conjecture" (Hobbling 45:23). The Qur'an had to overcome an overwhelming fatalism among the Arabs, who saw human frailty in contrast with the cold, irresistible force of time that swept all things away. Later in the same sura, the Qur'an exhorts Muhammad to respond: "Say, 'God gives you life then makes you die, then He shall gather you to the Day of Resurrection, wherein there is no doubt, but most men do not know'" (Hobbling 45:26).

Since the Qur'an is preaching resurrection to fatalist Arabs, it is careful to explain the logic of judgment. In the passage above, for instance, all unbelievers are forced to admit that they ignored the clear message of the prophets before they enter hell. Further, God's justice is described in terms easy for most people to understand: good labor on earth means good wages in heaven. These economic metaphors are found in other descriptions of Judgment Day, especially the great scales in which one's sins will be balanced against one's good deeds. These scales are mentioned several times in the Qur'an and were a popular topic in hadith collections. In the following passage, one theologian explains that a lifetime of sinful deeds will be outweighed by a single note containing the very confession of faith that the believer tries to say at the moment of death.

The common belief is that the scrolls on which the acts are written will be weighed in a balance which is provided with a needle and two platforms. All creatures will gaze on it, as it proceeds with equity and dismisses excuses; when it interrogates them concerning their acts, they will confess them with their tongues and bear witness to them in their limbs. This conception is corroborated by the tradition according to which man will be conducted to the balance; then nine and ninety seals to his debit will be opened, each of them [revealing a scroll] as long as sight reaches. Thereupon a note to his credit will be brought forth, containing the two phrases of the confession of faith ["there is no god but God and Muhammad is the prophet of God"]. Then the [scrolls] will be laid on one platform, and the note on the other; the [scrolls] will rise and the note will outweigh them.[12]

Popular stories have expanded upon the many images of Judgment Day found in the Qur'an. In some, the idea of the straight path (*sirat*) is developed into a bridge that crosses the chasm of hell, as exemplified in this account by a Swahili author:

How do the good souls find their way to the promised Garden? They will have to travel across the *sirat,* a mysterious structure spanning the long distance between the precipice below which is the seething crater of hell-fire and pitch black smoke, and on the other side, visible only faintly for the true believers, there is a bank of bliss, the shore of salvation, the hills of happiness. The distance is one of 3,000 years. Some very profound scholars have written that this abyss is the mouth of a gigantic serpent called Ghashiya in whose stomach God has placed the fires of hell, in order to protect his many delicate angels against its pestiferous fumes. When the serpent breathes, hot winds blow in Arabia. One hair of this monster lies across its mouth from lip to lip: that single hair is the *sirat,* the bridge across the abyss of hell-fire. For those whose sins are heavy, it will take 50,000 years to cross the hair-bridge and by the time they arrive they will be scorched black by the mountain-high flames sent up to torture them and to purify them. The souls of people who have given away all their wealth to the poor will find a white horse or a camel waiting for them, each with its owner's name written on its face. God created those shining animals out of the money which those kind souls gave to poor widows and orphans during their lives. The wise person who never sinned at all but prayed constantly will find a huge white bird that will take that individual across on its back in the time it takes to milk a cow. Whoever arrives on the other bank on the edge of the escarpment is safe.[13]

Other images used by the Qur'an to describe the awesome day include a book in which all deeds have been written. The soul will then be required to recognize this list of deeds to demonstrate that "no soul bears the burden of another" (17:14–15). Another common image is that of one's own body testifying against oneself, since God can ask a person's hands what deeds they have done and need not depend on a person's rationalization of these actions (41:19–22). Perhaps the most important image used to demonstrate God's ultimate right to judge is that of the primordial covenant, when God gathered all souls before the beginning of time and had them bear witness that he was God. This description is consistent with the Muslim belief that all creation, human beings included, is innately submissive to God's will, but unbelievers use their freedom of action to leave God's clear path.

> And when thy Lord took from the Children of Adam, from their loins, their seed, and made them testify touching themselves, "Am I not your Lord?" They said, "Yes, we testify"—lest you should say on the Day of Resurrection, "As for us, we were heedless of this."
> —The Battlements 7:17

All these images have a basic theology in common. First, God has a right to judge human beings for their acts. Not only is he their creator, but they bore witness to this fact on a day before time, and so to deny God is to deny their very nature. Second, God is a fair judge, capable of knowing the sum of one's actions; he can even cause a person's body to testify to doing actions that a person's mind might try to deny. Third, sins are a burden that weigh a person down both in this world and in the next. If the sins are especially heavy, they may tip the scales and consign a person to eternal hellfire, or they may cause a person to stumble when traversing the sirat, which stretches across the chasm of hell. Finally, a Muslim will obtain a special compensation for leading a pious life. Muhammad may intercede directly for his people, or the simple confession of faith may outweigh ninety-nine scrolls full of sins.

With such devastating images of judgment and hellfire, it is not surprising that some Muslim preachers have worried about people becoming too fixated on good and evil acts, instead of concentrating on the all-important intentions behind those acts. One famous mystic, Rabiᶜah al-ᶜAdawiyyah (d. 801), supposedly wandered the streets of Baghdad with a pitcher of water in one hand and a torch in another. Her purpose was to douse the flames of hell and set heaven on fire so that no Muslim would be motivated to commit actions out of fear or avarice. For Rabiᶜah, all acts must be done out of love for God.

Finally, the Muslim view of death reflects the Muslim view of life. Since life on this earth is seen as generally positive, death of a loved one can be a profound tragedy. Further, just as Muslims have a strong belief in the unseen world of angels and devils, they also differentiate between one's apparent actions and one's intentions. The pious soul who does good things for the love of God will gain a heavenly reward. In this way, a Muslim hopes to die during some act of devotion to God, whether this is struggling against some evil, undertaking the pilgrimage to Mecca, or simply confessing one's faith. God knows the difference between the true believer and the hypocrite and will judge on the basis of that knowledge.

The end of this world will be marked by a trumpet blast or a mighty cry, at which point all humankind will rise from the dead and be judged. Body will be united with soul, and each individual will be judged on the basis of his or her deeds alone, though Muhammad may offer some special intercession for his community. Each soul will be consigned either to heaven or to hell, which, though described in human terms, contains unimaginable bliss or unparalleled horrors.

This inevitable journey at the end of time is, paradoxically, often depicted as a return home—as if time were stretched out in a great bow with the two ends, creation and Judgment Day, at virtually the same point. A common refrain among Muslims at the loss of a loved one is "Surely we are from God and to God we shall return." This sentiment has its roots in the Qur'an itself, which calls out those words that every believer wants to hear:

O soul at peace,
return unto thy Lord, well-pleased and well-pleasing!
Enter thou among My servants!
Enter thou My paradise!

—The Dawn 89:27–30

CHAPTER 4

Christianity

BRUCE CHILTON

WHY ONE DIES AND HOW ONE DIES

Jesus pictured life with God as involving such a radical change that ordinary human relationships would no longer prevail. Because that change in all its comprehensiveness was finally to the good, death—an intrinsic part of the way God changes our lives—was portrayed, deliberately and explicitly, as an opportunity, not a misfortune. To lose one's life, Jesus said, is to save it (Matt. 16:25; Mark 8:35; Luke 9:24; John 12:25). That central assertion of Christianity is often treated as if it were poetic or paradoxical, but it expresses a core element around which Jesus' teaching as a whole was constructed.

Jesus' profound confidence in God's will to change us radically brought with it a commitment to the language of eschatology, of the ultimate transformation that God both promised and threatened. Although Jesus' eschatology was sophisticated, there is no mistaking his emphasis on future transformation.[1] Some efforts have been made recently to discount the eschatological dimension of Jesus' teaching; they have not prevailed. Periodically, theologians in the West have attempted to convert Jesus' perspective into their own sense that the world is a static and changeless entity, but that appears to have been far from his orientation.[2]

Although the eschatological character of Jesus' thinking is widely recognized, consensus is much more difficult to come by

79

when it concerns Jesus' understanding of what is to occur *to particular human beings* within God's disclosure of God's kingdom. Resurrection, as usually defined, promises actual life to individual persons within God's global transformation of all things. Because Jesus, on a straightforward reading of the Gospels, does not say much about resurrection as such, there has been a lively dispute over whether he had any distinctive (or even emphatic) teaching in that regard.

Still, when Jesus does address the issue, what he says is unequivocal. Sadducees are portrayed as asking a mocking question of Jesus, designed to disprove the possibility of resurrection.[3] Because Moses commanded that, were a man to die childless, his brother should raise up a seed for him, suppose there were seven brothers, the first of whom was married. If they all died childless in sequence, whose wife would the woman be in the resurrection (Matt. 22:23–28; Mark 12:18–23; Luke 20:27–33)?

Jesus' response is categorical and direct (following Mark 12:24–27; compare Matt. 22:29–32; Luke 20:34–38):

You completely deceive yourselves, knowing neither the Scriptures nor the power of God! Because when they arise from the dead, they neither marry nor are given in marriage, but are as angels in the heavens. But concerning the dead, that they rise, have you not read in the book of Moses about the bush, when God said to him, I am the God of Abraham and the God of Isaac and the God of Jacob? He is not God of the dead but of the living. You deceive yourselves greatly.

Two arguments are developed here, one from Scripture and one based on a comparison between angels and those who are resurrected. Of the two arguments, the one from Scripture is the more immediately fitting, an appeal both to the nature of God and to the evaluation of the patriarchs in early Judaism. If God identifies himself with Abraham, Isaac, and Jacob, it must be that in his sight, they live. And those three patriarchs—carefully chosen in Jesus' reflection—are living principles of Judaism itself; they are Israel as chosen in the case of Abraham (Gen. 15), as redeemed in the case of Isaac (Gen. 22), and as struggling to identity in the case of Jacob (Gen. 32). That evocation of patriarchal identity is implied, rather than demonstrated, but the assumption is that the hearer is able to make such connections between the text of Scripture and the fulfillment of that Scripture within present experience.[4] Yet that implicit logic of the argument from Scripture makes the second argument seem all the bolder by comparison.

The direct comparison between people in the resurrection and angels is consonant with the thought that the patriarchs must live in the sight of God, since angels are usually associated with God's throne (for example, in Dan. 7:9–14). Once the patriarchs are held to be alive before God, the comparison with angels is feasible. But Jesus' statement is not only a theoretical assertion of the majesty of God, a majesty that includes the patriarchs (and, by extension, the patriarchs' comparability to the angels); it is also an emphatic claim of what we might call divine anthropology. Jesus asserts that human relations, especially the usual basis of human society and divisions among people (namely, sexual identity), are radically altered in the resurrection.[5]

The teaching of a radical alteration at the point of death underscores that Christianity's hope is not of a survival or a reincarnation of some remnant of our personalities. Rather, death is understood to be a watershed, such that the current configuration of relationships and of reality is wiped away. Part of the transformation of this world into the kingdom of God is that, as Paul put, "the form of this world is passing away" (1 Cor. 7:31). That is not in any sense a fatalistic statement. Rather, Paul was appropriating Jesus' hopeful teaching about the eschatological transformation of all things. From that perspective, the death of the individual and the removal of the present form of the world point toward the new thing God is about to do with all of us.

It is for this reason that Christianity in principle does not differentiate between the types of death that come to people. To take to oneself the right to decide when death occurs, whether another's or one's own, cannot be endorsed because that is an attempt to legislate when God will act in relation to a human being. But except for that arrogance, all forms of death are opportunities for resurrection, even death on a cross.

The why and the how of death within the perspective of Christianity involve a fundamental reversal of what most people expect to find. Instead of a punishment, death is an opportunity; instead of a careful training for a peaceful departure as an ideal, the stark fact of a basic interruption of life is emphasized. That fundamental reversal, however, is in the service of the expectation of what occurs after death. A statement of Paul in his letter to the Philippians is classic (Phil. 1:21–24): "Because to me to live is Christ, and to die is gain. Yet if to live in flesh is the harvest of my work, I do not know what I shall choose. But I am constrained between the two, having a desire to leave and to be with Christ (very much better), but to remain in flesh (the more necessary for you)."

Philippians was probably written after Paul's death, but on the basis of the memory of what his companions remembered of his own mature positions and attitudes. In the present case, there is an exceptional clarity in regard to the actual focus of ethical striving within Christianity. The measure of the struggle is the spiritual inheritance that awaits the follower of Jesus rather than compensation in terms of this world. The actual purpose of being alive is to achieve spirit, and on that basis to know a life that is no longer limited to the flesh and the self. Death is the closure of that limited existence and therefore holds out the prospect of a complete transformation into the realm of spirit.

Within the Christian emphasis upon spiritual transformation, the sense of Christianity's teaching in regard to sin becomes plain. Paul wrote in his letter to the Romans (7:14–25):

> For we know that the law is spiritual; but I am of flesh, sold into slavery under sin. Because what I achieve I do not know: for what I do not want, this I accomplish, but what I hate is what I do. But if what I do not want is what I do, I agree that law is worthwhile. And now it is no longer I who achieve it, but sin dwelling in me. For I know that nothing good dwells in me, that is in my flesh, because to want lies within me, but to achieve the worthwhile does not. Because I do not do the good I want, but the evil which I do not want, this I accomplish. But if what I do not want is what I do, I am no longer achieving it, but the sin dwelling in me. Therefore I find this law: when I wish to do the worthwhile, the bad lies within me. Because I recognize the law of God by the inner man, but I see another law in my members, warring against the law of my mind and taking me prisoner by the law of sin which is in my members. I am a miserable person! Who will save me from the body of this death? Thanks to God through Christ Jesus our Lord. So therefore: I serve God's law with the mind, but with flesh sin's law.

The fact of human limitation is there all our lives, written in our failed projects of improvement. Paul understood this condition, not as the circumstance of an individual, tortured psychology, but as inherently human. In the very act of aspiring to what is good, people provoke a resistance in their midst that assures their failure.

Finally, this teaching became known as that of original (in the sense of inherent) sin. Christianity is frequently charged with being too pessimistic in its assessment of people for that reason. Yet a case can be made for the view that human history better accords with a teaching of inherent human sin than it does with faith in human progress. In fact, Augustine made just that argument (among others) in his classic work *The City of God*.[6] In the end, however, the Christian doctrine of original sin is not grounded in the observation of human behavior. Its ground is the eschatological hope of the transformation that is to come. The promise of grace, sealed by the Spirit of God and anticipating a glorious fulfillment, makes it apparent by contrast that, just as the form of this world is passing away, so our human complicity in the failures of this world is also to be transcended.

WHAT HAPPENS AFTER DEATH

Paul's classic discussion of the issue of the resurrection in First Corinthians 15 clearly represents his continuing commitment to the categorical understanding of the resurrection that Jesus initiated. The particular occasion of his teaching is the apparent denial of the resurrection on the part of some people in Corinth (1 Cor. 15:12): "How can some of you say that there is no resurrection of the dead?"[7] His address of that denial is, first of all, on the basis of the integrity of apostolic preaching. Indeed, Paul prefaces his question with the earliest extant catalog of the traditions regarding Jesus' resurrection (1 Cor. 15:1–11). That record makes it plain why so much variety within stories of the appearance of the risen Jesus in the Gospels was possible: reference is made to a separate appearance to Cephas, then to the Twelve, then to more than five hundred "brothers" (cf. Matt. 28:10!), then to James, then to "all the apostles," and then finally to Paul himself (vv. 5–8). The depth and range of that catalog enable Paul to press on to his first argument against the Corinthian denial of the resurrection (15:13–14): "But if there is no resurrection of the dead, neither has Christ been raised; and if Christ has not been raised, then our preaching is empty and your faith is empty!"

Paul expands on this argument in what follows (1 Cor. 15:15–19), but the gist of what he says in that section is as simple as what he says at first: faith in Jesus' resurrection logically requires our affirmation of the reality of resurrection generally. That may seem to be an argument entirely from hypothesis until we remember that Paul sees the moment when belief in Jesus occurs as the occasion of our reception of the Spirit of God (Gal. 4:4–6): "When the fullness of time came, God sent forth his Son, born from woman, born under law, so that he might redeem those under law, in order that we might obtain Sonship. And because you are sons, God sent the Spirit of his Son into your hearts, crying, 'Abba! Father!'" Because the Spirit in baptism is nothing other than the *living* Spirit of God's Son, Jesus' resurrection is attested by the very fact of the primordially Christian experience of faith. The availability of his Spirit shows that he has been raised from the dead. In addition, the preaching in his name formally claims his resurrection, so that to deny resurrection as a whole is to make the apostolic preaching into a lie: empty preaching, as Paul says, and therefore empty faith.

Paul's emphasis in this context on the spiritual integrity of the apostolic preaching, attested in baptismal experience, is coherent with Jesus' earlier claim that the Scriptures warrant the resurrection (since God is God of the living rather than of the dead). Implicitly, Paul accords the apostolic preaching the same sort of authority that Jesus attributed to the Scriptures of Israel. Paul also proceeds—in a manner comparable to Jesus' argument—to an argument on the basis of *the category of humanity* that the resurrection involves: he portrays Jesus as the first of those raised from the dead. Where Jesus himself had compared those to be resurrected to angels, Paul compares them to Jesus. His resurrection provides hope for the resurrection of the dead as a whole (1 Cor. 15:20–28).

That hope, Paul goes on to argue, permits the Corinthians themselves to engage in the practice of being baptized on behalf of the dead (15:29).[8] The practice assumes that, when the dead come to be raised, even if they have not been baptized during life, baptism on their behalf after their death will confer benefit. Similarly, Paul takes his own courage as an example of the hopeful attitude that must assume the resurrection of the dead as its ground: Why else would Christians encounter the dangers that they do (15:30–32)?

The claim of resurrection, then, does not involve only a hope based upon a reception of Spirit and the promise of Scripture (whether in the form of the Scriptures of Israel or the apostolic preaching). Resurrection as an actual hope impinges directly upon what we conceive becomes of persons as we presently know them after they have died. (And that, of course, will immediately influence our conception of people as they are now perceived and how we might engage with them.) Paul's argument therefore cannot and does not rest solely on assertions of the spiritual integrity of the biblical witness and the apostolic preaching. He must also spell out an anthropology of resurrection, such that the spiritual hope and the scriptural witness are worked out within the terms of reference of human experience.

Precisely when he does that in First Corinthians 15, Paul develops a Christian metaphysics. He does so by comparing people in the resurrection, not to angels, as Jesus himself had done, but—as we have seen—*to the resurrected Jesus.* And that comparison functions for Paul because Jesus is preached as raised from the dead and because, within the experience of baptism, Jesus is known as the living source of the Spirit of God.[9] Jesus as raised from the dead is the point of departure for Paul's thinking about the resurrection, and because his focus is a particular human being, his analysis of the resurrection is much more systematic than Jesus'.

Just as we saw in volume 1 of the Pilgrim Library of World Religions, in reference to First Corinthians:

> When Paul thinks of a person, he conceives of a body as composed of flesh. Flesh in his definition is physical substance, which varies from one created thing to another (for example, people, animals, birds, and fish; 1 Cor. 15:35–39). But in addition to being physical bodies, people are also what Paul calls a "psychic body," by which he means bodies with souls (1 Cor. 15:44. (Unfortunately, the phrase is wrongly translated in many modern versions, but its dependence on the noun for "soul" [*psukhê*] shows what the real sense is.)[10] In other words, people as bodies are not just lumps of flesh, but they are self-aware. That self-awareness is precisely what makes them "psychic body."

Now in addition to being physical body and psychic body, Paul says we are (or can become) "spiritual body" (1 Cor. 15:44). That is, we can relate thoughts and feelings *to one another and to God,* as 1 Corinthians 2 has already shown us. Jesus is therefore the last Adam, a "life-giving spirit" (1 Cor. 15:45), just as the first Adam was a "living being" or "soul" (the two words are the same in Greek, *psukhê*). Jesus is the basis on which we can realize our identities as God's children, the brothers and sisters of Christ, and know the power of the resurrection.

The metaphysics of both Christology and spirituality are the same: they relate Christ to creation and believers to God, because in each the principle is the eschatological transformation of human nature by means of spirit. "Flesh" and "soul" become, not ends in themselves, but way stations on the course to "Spirit."

Just as sin marks out the necessity of human transformation in the realm of ethics, so physical death marks out the necessity of human transformation in the realm of its medium of existence. When Paul describes that existential transformation, his thinking becomes openly and irreducibly metaphysical (1 Cor. 15:35–44):

> But someone will say, How are the dead raised, and with what sort of body do they come? Fool, what you yourself sow does not become alive unless it dies! And what do you sow? You sow not the body which shall be, but a bare seed, perhaps of wheat or of another grain. But God gives to it a body just as he wills, and to each of the germs its own body. Not all flesh is the same flesh, but there is one of men, another flesh of animals, another flesh of birds, another of fish. And there are heavenly bodies and earthly bodies, but one is the glory of the heavenly and another of the earthly. One glory is the sun's and another the moon's, and another glory of stars, because star differs from star in glory. So also is the resurrection of the dead. Sown in corruption, it is raised in incorruption; sown in dishonor, it is raised in glory; sown in weakness, it is raised in power; sown a physical body, it is raised a spiritual body.

There is not a more exact statement of the process of resurrection in the whole of Christian literature, and Paul's words have had a firm place in Christian liturgies of burial. Their particular genius is the insight that resurrection involves a new creative act by God, what Paul elsewhere calls a "new creation" (2 Cor. 5:17; Gal. 6:15). But God's new creation is not simply an event that commences at death. Rather, a progressive transformation joins the realm of ethics together with the realm of metaphysics. Morally and existentially, the hope of the resurrection involves a fresh, fulfilled humanity.

RESURRECTION, NOT REINCARNATION

Born in 185 in Egypt, Origen knew the consequences that faith could have in the Roman world: his father died in the persecution of Severus in 202. Origen accepted the sort of renunciation

demanded of apostles in the Gospels, putting aside his posses-
sions to develop what Eusebius calls the philosophical life demanded by Jesus (Eusebius, *History of the Church* 6.3). His
learning resulted in his appointment to the catechetical school
in Alexandria, following the great examples of Pantaenus and
Clement. Origen later moved to Caesarea in Palestine as a result
of a bitter dispute with Demetrius, the bishop of Alexandria.
Origen remained a controversial figure after his death (and until this day), to a large extent because he wrestled more profoundly than most thinkers with the consequences of Spirit's
claim on the flesh.

In his treatment of the resurrection, Origen shows himself a
brilliant exegete and a profound theologian. He sees clearly
that, in First Corinthians 15, Paul insists that the resurrection
from the dead must be bodily. And Origen provides the logical
grounding of Paul's claim (Origen, *On First Principles* 2.10.1):
"If it is certain that we are to be possessed of bodies, and if those
bodies that have fallen are declared to rise again—and the expression 'rise again' could not properly be used except of that
which had previously fallen—then there can be no doubt that
these bodies rise again in order that at the resurrection we may
once more be clothed with them."

But Origen equally insists upon Paul's assertion that "flesh
and blood can not inherit the kingdom of God" (1 Cor. 15:50).
There must be a radical transition from flesh to spirit, as God
fashions a body that can dwell in the heavens (*On First Principles* 2.10.3).

Origen pursues the point of this transition into a debate
with other Christians (*On First Principles* 2.10.3):

We now direct the discussion to some of our own people, who either from want of intellect or from lack of instruction introduce
an exceedingly low and mean idea of the resurrection of the body.
We ask these men in what manner they think that the "psychic

body" will, by the grace of the resurrection be changed and become "spiritual"; and in what manner they think that what is sown "in dishonor" is to "rise in glory," and what is sown "in corruption" is to be transformed into "incorruption." Certainly if they believe the Apostle, who says that the body, when it rises in glory and in power and in incorruptibility, has already become spiritual, it seems absurd and contrary to the meaning of the Apostle to say that it is still entangled in the passions of flesh and blood.

Origen's emphatic denial of a physical understanding of the resurrection is especially interesting for two reasons. First, his confidence in the assertion attests the strength of his conviction that such an understanding is "low and mean": the problem is not that physical resurrection is unbelievable, but that the conception is unworthy of the hope that faith relates to. Origen's argument presupposes, of course, that a physical understanding of the resurrection was current in Christian Alexandria. But he insists, again following Paul's analysis, that the body that is raised in resurrection is continuous with the physical body in principle, but different from it in substance (*On First Principles* 2.10.3):

> So our bodies should be supposed to fall like a grain of wheat into the earth, but implanted in them is the cause that maintains the essence of the body. Although the bodies die and are corrupted and scattered, nevertheless by the word of God that same cause that has all along been safe in the essence of the body raises them up from the earth and restores and refashions them, just as the power that exists in a grain of wheat refashions and restores the grain, after its corruption and death, into a body with stalk and ear. And so in the case of those who shall be counted worthy of obtaining an inheritance in the kingdom of heaven, the cause before mentioned, by which the body is refashioned, at the order of God refashions out of the earthly and animate body a spiritual body, which can dwell in heaven.

The direction and orientation of Origen's analysis are defined by his concern to describe what in humanity may be regarded as ultimately compatible with the Divine. For that reason, physical survival is rejected as an adequate category for explaining the resurrection. Instead, he emphasizes the change of substance that must be involved.

Second, the force behind Origen's assertion is categorical. The resolution of the stated contradictions—"psychic"/"spiritual," "dishonor"/"glory," "corruption"/"incorruption"—involves taking Paul's language as directly applicable to the human condition. In the case of each contradiction, the first item in the pair needs to yield to the spiritual progression of the second item in the pair. That is the progressive logic of Origen's thought, now applied comprehensively to human experience.

In Origen's articulation, progressive thinking insists upon the radical transition that resurrection involves. Although his discussion is a brilliant exegesis of Paul's argument, Origen also elevates the progressive principle above any other consideration that Paul introduces. Paul had used this kind of method for understanding Scripture (Gal. 4:21–31), but in Origen's thought that approach is turned into the fundamental principle of global spiritual revolution. Only that, in his mind, can do justice to the promise of being raised from the dead.

For all that the transition from flesh to spirit is radical, Origen is also clear that personal continuity is involved. To put the matter positively, one is clothed bodily with one's own body, as we have already seen. To put the matter negatively, sins borne by the body of flesh may be thought of as visited upon the body, which is raised from the dead (*On First Principles* 2.10.8):

> Just as the saints will receive back the very bodies in which they have lived in holiness and purity during their stay in the habitations of this life, but bright and glorious as a result of the resurrection, so, too, the impious, who in this life have loved the darkness

of error and the night of ignorance will after the resurrection be clothed with murky and black bodies, in order that this very gloom of ignorance, which in the present world has taken possession of the inner parts of their mind, may in the world to come be revealed through the garment of their outward body.

Although Origen is quite consciously engaging in speculation at this point, he firmly rejects the notion that the flesh is involved in the resurrection, even when biblical promises appear to envisage earthly joys (*On First Principles* 2.11.2):

> Now some men, who reject the labor of thinking and seek after the outward and literal meaning of the law, or rather give way to their own desires and lusts, disciples of the mere letter, consider that the promises of the future are to be looked for in the form of pleasure and bodily luxury. And chiefly on this account they desire after the resurrection to have flesh of such a sort that they will never lack the power to eat and drink and to do all things that pertain to flesh and blood, not following the teaching of the Apostle Paul about the resurrection of a "spiritual body."

His reasons for rejecting such a millenarian view are both exegetical and theological. Paul is the ground of the apostolic authority he invokes, in a reading we have already seen. He uses that perspective to consider the Scriptures generally (*On First Principles* 2.11.3). But Origen deepens his argument from interpretation with a profoundly theological argument. He maintains that the most urgent longing is the desire "to learn the design of those things which we perceive to have been made by God." This longing is as basic to the mind as the eye is to the body: constitutionally, we long for the vision of God (*On First Principles* 2.11.4).

The manner in which Origen develops his own thought is complex, involving a notion of education in paradise prior to one's entry into the realm of heaven proper (*On First Principles* 2.11.6):

> I think that the saints when they depart from this life will remain in some place situated on the earth, which the divine Scripture calls "paradise." This will be a place of learning and, so to speak, a lecture room or school for souls, in which they may be taught about all that they had seen on earth and may also receive some indication of what is to follow in the future. Just as when placed in this life they had obtained certain indications of the future, seen indeed "through a glass darkly," and yet truly seen "in part," they are revealed more openly and clearly to the saints in the proper places and times. If anyone is of truly pure heart and of clean mind and well-trained understanding he will make swifter progress and quickly ascend to the region of the air,[11] until he reaches the Kingdom of heaven, passing through the series of those "mansions," if I may so call them, which the Greeks have termed spheres—that is, globes—but which the divine Scripture calls heavens.

Even this brief excerpt from a convoluted description represents the complexity of Origen's vision, but two factors remain plain and simple. First, the vision of God is the moving element through the entire discussion. Second, Origen clearly represents and develops a construction of the Christian faith in which eschatology has been swallowed up in an emphasis upon transcendence. The only time that truly matters is the time until one's death, which determines one's experience in paradise and in the resurrection. "Heaven" as cosmographic place now occupies the central position once occupied by the eschatological kingdom of God in Jesus' teaching. That, too, occurs on the authority of progressive dialectics, the refinement of Pauline metaphysics.

Unlike Origen, Augustine refutes the Manichaean philosophy that he accepted prior to his conversion to Christianity. In

Manichaeanism, named after a Persian teacher of the third century named Mani, light and darkness are two eternal substances that struggle against each other, and they war over the creation they have both participated in making.[12] As in the case of Gnosticism, on which it was dependent, Manichaeanism counseled a denial of the flesh. By his insistence on the resurrection of the flesh, Augustine revives the strong assertion of the extent of God's embrace of his own creation (in the tradition of Irenaeus, the great millenarian thinker of the second century).[13]

At the same time, Augustine sets a limit on the extent to which one might have recourse to Plato. Augustine had insisted with Plato against the Manichaeans that God was not a material substance, but transcendent. Consequently, evil became in his mind the denial of what proceeds from God (*Confessions* 5.10.20). When it came to the creation of people, however, Augustine insisted against Platonic thought that no division between soul and flesh could be made (*City of God* 22.12). Enfleshed humanity was the only genuine humanity, and God in Christ was engaged to raise those who were of the city of God. Moreover, Augustine specifically refuted the contention of Porphyry (and Origen) that cycles of creation could be included within the entire scheme of salvation. For Augustine, the power of the resurrection within the world as it is was already confirmed by the miracles wrought by Christ and his martyrs. He gives the example of the healings connected with the relics of Saint Stephen, recently transferred to Hippo (*City of God* 22.8).

Even now, in the power of the Catholic Church, God is represented on earth, and the present, Christian epoch (*Christiana tempora*) corresponds to the millennium promised in Revelation 20 (*City of God* 20.9). This age of dawning power, released in flesh by Jesus and conveyed by the church, awaits the full transition into the city of God, complete with flesh itself. It is telling that, where Origen could cite a saying of Jesus to confirm his view of the resurrection (see Matt. 22:30; Mark 12:25; Luke 20:36), Augustine has to qualify the meaning of the same saying (*City of God* 22.18): "They will be equal to angels in immortality and happiness, not in flesh, nor indeed in resurrection, which the angels had no need of, since they could not die. So the Lord said that there would be no marriage in the resurrection, not that there would be no women."

In all of this, Augustine is straining, although he is usually a less convoluted interpreter of Scripture. But he is committed to what the Latin version of the Apostles' Creed promises: "the resurrection of the flesh" and all that implies. He therefore cannot follow Origen's exegesis.

A double irony is here. First, Origen, the sophisticated allegorist, seems much simpler to follow in his exegesis of Jesus' teaching than Augustine, the incomparable preacher. Second, Augustine's discussion of such issues as the fate of fetuses in the resurrection sounds remarkably like the Sadducees' hypothesis that Jesus argues against in the relevant passage from the synoptic Gospels.

Augustine is well aware, as was Origen before him, that Paul speaks of a "spiritual body" and acknowledges that "I suspect that all utterance published concerning it is rash." And yet he can be quite categorical that flesh must be involved somehow: "The spiritual flesh will be subject to spirit, but it will still be flesh, not spirit; just as the carnal spirit was subject to the flesh, but was still spirit, not flesh" (*City of God* 22.21). Such is Augustine's conviction that flesh has become the medium of salvation now and hereafter.

CONCLUSION

Not only within the New Testament, but through the centuries of discussion that the key figures cited here reflect, Christianity represents itself as a religion of human regeneration. Humanity is regarded not simply as a quality that God values, but as the very center of human being in the image of God. That center is so precious to God, it is the basis upon which it is possible for human beings to enter the kingdom of God, both now and eschatologically.

The medium in which the ultimate transformation is to take place is a matter of debate. Regenerated people might be compared to angels (so Jesus), to Jesus in his resurrection (so Paul), to spiritual bodies (so Origen), and to spiritualized flesh (so Augustine). But in all of these analyses of how we are to be transformed into the image of Christ so as to apprehend the humanity that is in the image and likeness of God (Gen. 1:27), there is a fundamental consensus. Jesus is claimed as the agency by which this transformation is accomplished.

CHAPTER 5

Hinduism

BRIAN K. SMITH

A mong all the many reasons why human beings have conceived, preserved, and relied upon religion, the intractable
problem of the inevitability of death surely must be among the
most powerful. Few of us find comfort in the prospect that this
short life is all there is, or that death terminates what we call the
"self" or "soul." Religions of all sorts have provided alternatives
to this kind of nihilism by holding out the guarantee of continued existence after death—an "afterlife." They have also linked
the afterlife to this life in ways that bolster the ritual, moral, and
ethical systems put forward by particular traditions. Rewards
and punishments for adherence to and noncompliance with
these codes of conduct and belief are projected into the future.
In most religions, the afterlife is in one way or another the
causal product of the type of life lived in this world.

In Indian religions (Buddhism, Jainism, and others, as well
as Hinduism), this linkage has been assumed for millennia.
Even in the earliest historical period of Indian history, Vedic
thinkers, philosophers, and ritualists assumed a connection between religious acts of sacrifice and the supposed results of such
acts not only in this life but also in an afterlife in heaven. By the
middle centuries of the first millennium B.C.E., such a theory of
relations between ritual acts (*karma*) and their "fruits" was ex-
tended to *all* acts. Every action performed in this life carried
with it consequences in the future—good or bad, pleasant or
unpleasant. Furthermore, this theory of moral cause and effect,

sometimes referred to as "the law of karma," posited future existences not only in a heaven or hell but also rebirth (of various
sorts) in this world, and all such rebirths were seen as correlated
to one's past karma.

Hinduism, from this time onward, has in all its forms assumed transmigration and rebirth guided by the particular
karma produced by the individual in his or her past. Death here
is certainly not final; birth, life, death, and rebirth are stages in
the endless cycle of existence called *samsara*.

For Hinduism, then, the problem is not so much death itself
as it is continual, perpetual, and potentially eternal rebirth.
Hindus, no less than anyone else, fear death and are concerned
with their future prospects after death. Hinduism takes for
granted rebirth and offers its adherents ways to favorably affect
the conditions they will face in the afterlife. Ultimately, however, Hinduism also offers an alternative to the endless cycle
of rebirth. Through the cultivation of various methods, Hindus
believe it is possible to obtain a state of "release" or "liberation"
from samsara, an eternal and changeless state of salvation that
not only overcomes death but also frees one from continual
rebirth.

WHY ONE DIES AND HOW ONE DIES
(A GOOD DEATH, SUICIDE)

Generally speaking, Hindu texts pay relatively little attention to
the question of why there is death or how death came to be part
of life in the first place. Like evil, death is regarded as an unfortunate but necessary element of a universe consisting of the
"pairs of opposites"—good and evil, life and death, up and
down, and so forth.[1] Rather than obsess about why one dies,
Hinduism concentrates more on how to live in order to obtain
a favorable afterlife and rebirth or, even more preferably, how to
escape the process of death and rebirth altogether.

There are, however, myths of origins that explore the question of how death (often equated with evil) was introduced into the world. Many of these stories assume that human beings were originally immortal, that is, godlike. In virtually every case, death is instituted not as punishment for any sort of "original sin," as in the major Western religions. Rather, in many myths the origin of mortality is represented as either a practical or a metaphysical necessity or as an inducement for humans to live a righteous life.

The origin of death is portrayed in the following text in very pragmatic terms. If all creatures lived forever, the earth would become overpopulated and weighted down with inhabitants. Death is introduced to lighten the earth's load:

> Formerly, in the Golden Age, when there was no fear or danger, the eternal, primeval god (Adideva) acted as Yama (the god of death), and while he did so no one died, but people continued to be born. All creatures increased, birds and cows and horses and wild animals, and men increased by the millions. This dangerous crowd overburdened the Earth, who sought refuge with Vishnu. He said, "Do not worry. I will see to it that you are lightened."[2]

God's invention of death thus depopulates the overburdened earth. The myth suggests the obvious: if everyone lived forever, the earth could not sustain all beings. Death is thus represented as a practical necessity for the sustaining of life.

In another myth, time (in the form of "the year" and also identified with Prajapati, the "lord of creatures" and creator god) is said to be death, and even the gods fear him. But while Prajapati imparts to the gods the means for obtaining immortality, the god of death (Mrtyu, "Death") becomes concerned that he will have "no share" if human beings also possess such skills and also become immortal:

The year is death, for he destroys the life of mortal beings by means of night and day, then they die. The gods were afraid of this (god) Prajapati (who is) the year, death, the ender, for they feared that he would put an end to their lives. They performed sacrifices but they did not attain immortality. They continued to exert themselves, and Prajapati taught them the proper ritual to perform, so that they became immortal. Then Death said to the gods, "Surely in this way all men will become immortal, and then what will be my share?" The gods said that the body would not be immortal but would be the share of death, while the rest of the man who had achieved immortality through knowledge or ritual acts would become immortal.[3]

Immortality is here assured for human beings who have cultivated mystical knowledge or who have mastered the sacrificial ritual. But at the same time, Death is given his share in the form of the physical body. While the soul may escape the hands of Death, the body will never do so henceforth. This myth also implies that death creates and maintains the necessary distinctions between immortal gods and mortal humans. While human beings, too, can become godlike through their own efforts, the death of the body is always a precursor.

In yet another story of origins, death is introduced as an incentive to keep human beings focused on religion. Brahma, the god of creation, appoints Rudra (who is also known as Siva) to bring forth creatures. Rudra does his duty well, producing beings who were "great ascetics," wholly righteous and spiritually powerful, and thus capable of achieving immortality through their own efforts. "When Brahma saw them he asked Siva to create instead beings who would be subject to death, for, said Brahma, 'Creatures free from death will not undertake actions or holy rituals.'"[4] Death here is depicted as the motivation for human goodness: in light of the inevitability of death, human beings will behave themselves and practice religion in order to be saved from it.

More often than not, rather than trying to explain why death occurs, Hinduism simply assumes its existence. "Death is inevitable in the case of the man who is born," as it is phrased in one text. "Therefore, one should not be happy at birth, nor mourn death. A creature comes from the unknown and goes to the unknown; so the wise regard birth and death as equal."[5] This kind of equanimity in the face of death is one kind of ideal for how to die a "good death" and is obviously the product of a life in which such equanimity and wisdom have been cultivated through long training.

Another strategy for "dying well" assumes that one's afterlife is determined by the dying person's last thought (a theory also embraced by Tibetan Buddhism). "Whatever being (or object) he remembers when he abandons the body at death, he enters, Arjuna, always existing in that being." Thus, for example, fixing one's mind on God at one's final moment of life will deliver one to God in the afterlife: "Therefore, at all times remember me . . . mind and understanding fixed on me, free from doubt, you will come to me."[6] Again, having the wherewithal to consciously fix upon a favorable last thought at the time of death requires a lifetime of preparation.

Yet another practice that is found, albeit rarely, in the Hindu tradition is religious suicide. The world renouncer, who has already "died to the world," can willingly give up his physical body in order to obtain salvation, according to some texts. Another, and infamous, case of religious suicide is *sati,* the self-sacrifice of a widow who follows her recently departed husband to the afterlife by entering into her own funereal pyre.[7] Although such practices are part of the Hindu tradition of how to die a "good death," other texts warn against them: "One ought not to yield to his own desire and pass away before (he has attained) the full extent of life, for such does not make for the heavenly world" (Satapatha Brahmana 10.2.6.7).

The death of the good man, who is helped along his journey by virtue of his meritorious acts in this life, is in the following passage contrasted to that of the unrighteous. The former obtains an easy death and passes on with minimal distress; the latter, however, undergoes quite a different experience:

> If a man has been habitually generous about giving water and food and liquids, all that he has given now brings him refreshment in his moment of distress. A man who gave food with a mind purified by faith now becomes satisfied even without any food at all. And if a man has never told lies, or ruined anyone else's pleasure, and if he is a faithful believer in the gods, he experiences an easy death. People who have always taken pleasure in worshiping gods and Brahmins, and who have never envied others, who have spoken fairly and been generous and modest, those men die happy. A man who has never abandoned dharma (righteousness or duty) because of lust or rashness or hatred, who has done as he is told and is gentle, he finds an easy death. But men who have not been donors of water or food find burning thirst and hunger when the time of their death comes upon them. People who have given money overcome cold; those who have given sandalwood paste overcome heat; and those who have never caused anyone any distress overcome the painful suffering that destroys the vital breath. Those who have caused delusion and ignorance find great fear, and the worst men are oppressed by terrible torments. A false witness, a liar, and a man who teaches wrong things, they all die in delirium, and so do those who revile the Vedas.[8]

The actual process of death and dying has been analyzed in many of the Hindu scriptures. Most assume that the basic constituents of the human body are correlated to the fundamental elements of nature, and upon the death of the body return to whence they came—ashes to ashes, dust to dust. The human body is thus a kind of microcosm, and at the time of death dissipates back into the macrocosm. In the following, the student queries his teacher about what survives once the body and its faculties are dispersed into the universe upon death:

> "Yajnavalkya," Artabhaga said again, "tell me—when a man has died, and his speech disappears into fire, his breath into the wind, his sight into the sun, his mind into the moon, his hearing into the quarters, his physical body into the earth, his self into space, the hair of his body into plants, the hair of his head into trees, and his blood and semen into water—what then happens to that person?"
> —Brhadaranyaka Upanishad 3.2.13[9]

Other texts answer this question by positing the existence of a "subtle body" or essential self or soul called the *jiva,* which survives death. The jiva, here said to be in the "form of a man the size of a thumb," endures the dissolution of the body at death:

> Earth, wind, sky, fire and water—these are the seed of the body of all who have bodies. The body made of these five elements is an artificial and impermanent thing which turns to ashes. The jiva has the form of a man the size of a thumb; this subtle body is taken on in order to experience (the fruits of karma). That subtle body does not turn to ashes even in the blazing fire in hell; it is not destroyed in water, even after a long time, nor by weapons, swords or missiles, nor by very sharp thorns or heated iron or stone, or by the embrace of a heated image, or even by a fall from a very high place. It is not burnt or broken.[10]

There is no one, standardized theory in Hinduism about what happens to this soul after the death of the body. Most strands of Hinduism have adopted the theory of karma and rebirth, arguing that one's future destiny is determined by one's acts in this and past lives. Under this conception, a person is held responsible for the type of afterlife he or she receives. But many Hindus also believe that the deceased's survivors have a responsibility for helping the recently departed along the way. Death rites, performed ideally by the eldest son under the supervision of specialized priests, begin with cremation, at which time the skull is cracked in order to free the soul. Rituals involving the offering of rice balls, food, and gifts continue at intervals for a year, and are designed to transform the spirit (*preta*) into an ancestor (*pitr*). "The dead man does not immediately after his death and without more ado join the number of the ancestors who are worshiped," notes one scholar; "on the contrary fixed ceremonies are necessary for elevating the deceased to the rank of ancestors."[11]

Death rites are thus conceived of as a kind of last sacrifice to the gods (in which the body is the offering) and as a rebirth or transformation of the dead into a new life as an ancestor. But they also serve to ease the pain and discomfort of the recently departed and nourish the disembodied spirit:

> When his corpse is being burnt, he experiences terrible burning; and when it is beaten he suffers too, and when it is cut he suffers intense agony. When a man('s body) stays wet for a very long time he suffers miserably, even if by the ripening of his own karma he has gone to another body. But whatever water, together with sesamum seeds, his relatives offer (in the rites for dead relatives), and whatever balls of rice they offer, he eats that as he is being led along. When his relatives rub his (dead) body with oil and massage his limbs, that nourishes and strengthens a man, and so does whatever his relatives eat. A dead man who does not (take the form of a ghost) and bother his relatives on earth too much when they are asleep and dreaming is nourished and strengthened by them as they give him gifts (in the form of offerings to his departed soul).[12]

The newly created ancestor, however, is thought to be capable of taking on a new existence in one of the many Hindu heavens or hells, from which one is again reborn, or becomes reincarnated in this world more or less immediately. Views of the afterlife are complex and varied, but in all cases are closely linked to the past karma of the individual.

WHAT HAPPENS AFTER DEATH

Even in the earliest period of the history of Hinduism, one's future was said to be determined by past actions. In the Vedic era, however, "good" actions—or karma—which resulted in a pleasant afterlife were defined as ritual actions. Given the emphasis on the regular performance of sacrificial rituals, the Vedic texts assert that a "divine self" that one assumes in a heavenly world is the product of the rituals one performs in this life. The divine self is said to be "born out of the sacrifice," that is, it is a ritual construct: "The sacrifice becomes the sacrificer's self in yonder world. And truly, the sacrificer who, knowing this, performs that (sacrifice) comes into existence (there) with a whole body" (Satapatha Brahmana 11.1.8.6). Another text declares that the sacrificer "is united in the other world with what he has sacrificed" (Taittiriya Samhita 3.3.85), and yet another declares, "Whatever oblation he sacrifices here, that becomes his self in the other world. When he who knows this leaves this world, the offering which follows him calls out, 'Come here. Here I am, your self'" (Satapatha Brahmana 11.2.2.5).

Upon death, a kind of judgment occurs. Good deeds and bad ones are separated out and weighed, and the newly deceased follows whichever rises in the scale to his destiny: "For in yonder world they place him on the scale, and whichever of the two rises that he will follow, whether it be the good or the evil. And whoever knows this gets on the scale even in this world, and escapes being put on the scale in yonder world. For his good action rises, not his bad action" (Satapatha Brahmana 11.2.7.33).

For those whose good acts (i.e., ritual performances) outweigh the bad, an immortal life in a heavenly world is promised. Some texts attempt to locate the distance of heaven from earth: one claims it is the equivalent distance of a thousand cows standing one on top of the other (Pancavimsa Brahmana 16.8.6), while another states that its distance is equal to a thousand-days' journey on horseback (Pancavimsa Brahmana 16.10.3). The Vedas depict this heaven as a world of light, sometimes equated with the sun, in which every kind of happiness is abundantly provided: milk, honey, ghee, and liquor flow freely; the sound of singing and the flute is in the air; and all desires are fulfilled. Heaven is a place where the pleasant things of this life are found in unlimited quantities and are enjoyed forever.

Conversely, the Vedas describe various hells to which evildoers and those negligent of their sacrificial duties are consigned. Those who spit on a Brahmin, or flick the mucus of their nose on him, will spend their afterlife sitting in a stream of blood, devouring their hair for food (Atharva Veda 5.19.3). Those who consume food in this world without first sacrificing some of it to the gods will enter one of a variety of hells where revenge is exacted: "For whatever food a man eats in this world, by the very same is he eaten again in the other" (Satapatha Brahmana 12.9.1.1).

The myth of Bhrgu,[13] son of Varuna, tells of a young man's journey to the other world and the sights he sees there. The story literalizes the notion of retribution in the next life at the hands of what one kills and eats in this life, and emphasizes the salvific power of sacrificial action:

> Bhrgu arrived in the world beyond. There he saw a man cut another man to pieces and eat him. He said, "Has this really hap-

pened? What is this?" They said to him, "Ask Varuna, your father. He will tell you about this." He came to a second world, where a man was eating another man, who was screaming. He said, "Has this really happened? What is this?" They said to him, "Ask Varuna, your father. He will tell you about this." He went on to another world, where he saw a man eating another man, who was soundlessly screaming. . . . In (yet another) world there were five rivers with blue lotuses and white lotuses, flowing with honey like water. In them there were dancing and singing, the sound of the lute, crowds of celestial nymphs, a fragrant smell, and a great sound.

Bhrgu returns from the other world and queries his father about the meaning of these various sights. Varuna tells him that the afterlife in which men cut other men into pieces and eat them is for those in this world who "offer no oblation and lack true knowledge, but cut down trees and lay them on the fire," for "those trees take the form of men in the other world and eat (those people) in return." One can avoid this fate by putting fuel on the sacred fire in the course of sacrifice. The second sight, in which men eat other men who are screaming, is for those who eat animals outside of the sacrificial context (the animals, who scream at death, take on the form of men in the next world). One escapes this destiny by, again, offering sacrifice. Men who devour others who are "soundlessly screaming" in the other world are, similarly, the form in the afterlife rice and barley take when eaten in this world outside the confines of the ritual; it too is avoided by proper sacrifice. The world of lotuses is for those who sacrifice correctly: "There is no chance of getting (these good) worlds except by the sacrifice. . . . Whoever offers the oblation with this true knowledge, he is not eaten in return by trees who take the form of men in the other world, nor by animals, nor by rice and barley."

In the later Vedic period, ritualists and philosophers begin to speak of the possibility of a "re-death" from the heavenly world sacrificial acts procure. If life in heaven is the product of one's ritual acts, and if there is a finite number of such acts one can perform in this life, what happens to the individual enjoying heaven when the merit of his acts wears out? Can one "die again" from the heavenly world, and if so, what happens next to the individual? Such thinking perhaps led to the development of the full-blown theory of karma and rebirth as it is first found in the Upanishads and subsequently becomes integral to Hinduism. The theory assumes what the earlier Vedic ritualists had already posited—that one's future is the consequence of one's past and present acts—but expands the notion of cause and effect to *all* action, not just ritual action. Furthermore, it traces the source of karma, and thus of rebirth, which is fueled and shaped by karma, to desire:

> What a man turns out to be depends on how he acts and on how he conducts himself. If his actions are good, he will turn into something good. If his actions are bad, he will turn into something bad. A man turns into something good by good action and into something bad by bad action. And so people say: "A person here consists simply of desire." A man resolves in accordance with his desire, acts in accordance with his resolve, and turns out to be in accordance with his action.[14]

Desire, resolve, and action (the components of karma) direct the course of an individual's future life both in this lifetime and in subsequent births. But it is also emphasized that, for "a man who's attached" to desire and action, rebirth is perpetual:

> *A man who's attached goes with his action,*
> *to that very place to which*
> *his mind and character cling.*
> *Reaching the end of his action,*

of whatever he has done in this world—
From that world he returns
back to this world,
back to action.

—Brhadaranyaka Upanishad 4.4.6

From the time of the Upanishads onward, the earlier theory of an afterlife in heaven or hell is combined with the notion that one also is eventually reborn again on earth. In many texts of Hinduism it appears as though the individual undergoes a kind of double retribution, first in another world of reward or punishment and then again in the type of rebirth one receives in this world. For the virtuous—those who engage in good actions here on earth—heaven is assured, but rebirth is also inevitable when the karmic merit of their actions that won them a place in the heavenly world is exhausted:

> Men learned in sacred lore, soma drinkers, their sins absolved, worship me with sacrifices, seeking to win heaven. Reaching the holy world of Indra, king of the gods, they savor the heavenly delights of the gods in the celestial sphere. When they have long enjoyed the world of heaven and their merit is exhausted, they enter the mortal world; following the duties ordained in sacred lore, desiring desires, they obtain what is transient.
>
> —Bhagavad Gita 9.20–21

Heavens and hells, often depicted in detailed imaginative terms, are not permanent states but function as transient and intermediate way stations as one moves along one's way toward the next rebirth. As in the case cited above of Bhrgu's journey to the other world, the heavenly and hellish realms described in later Hindu texts are often places in which the rewards and punishments experienced there exactly correlate to the virtuous or evil deeds committed in this lifetime. The text below delineates a series of sufferings in hell for those who have sinned in their lives on earth:

> Those sinners who have constantly condemned the Vedas, gods, or brahmins, those who have ignored the beneficial teachings of Purana and Itihasa, those who find fault with their teacher, who obstruct sacred feasts, who hinder donors, all these fall into these hells. Wicked people who provoke dissension between friends, between husband and wife, between brothers, between master and servant, father and son, sacrificer and teacher, and those dishonorable men who give their daughter to one man having already given her to another—all these are split in two by Yama's (the god of death's) servants with a saw. . . . The foolish man who refuses food, eating elsewhere when invited to the *sraddha* (sacrificial feast) for gods and ancestors, is bitten in two by large sharp-beaked birds. Battering them with their beaks, birds alight on those who strike good men in vulnerable spots and abuse them with words. One who is hypocritically slanderous to good men suffers huge birds with horny beaks and claws who pull out his tongue. Those haughty people who treat their mothers, fathers, and teachers with contempt go to hell where they lie with their faces downward in pus, feces and urine.[15]

After a period of time, the merit or demerit that brought the individual to such an afterlife is used up, and the soul is propelled once more into yet another life, again determined by past karma. Such a cycle of death, rebirth, and death again—driven by karma produced by desire—is called *samsara,* and is contrasted to the eternal, changeless, and blissful state in which there is no rebirth of any kind, *moksa* or "liberation." Rebirth on earth (immediately or after the intermediary period of reward and retribution in heaven or hell) can take many forms, pleasant or unpleasant, but is thought to be continuous until the cycle is broken.

RESURRECTION AND REINCARNATION

"Just as the embodied self (in this lifetime) enters childhood, youth, and old age," says the Bhagavad Gita, "so does it enter another body; this does not confound the steadfast man" (Bhagavad Gita 2.13). This process of rebirth or reincarnation is analyzed in different ways in different Hindu texts. Among the earliest theories is the "five fires doctrine," which conceives of the procedure as a series of sacrificial offerings into various "fires" (see Brhadaranyaka Upanishad 6.2.9–13; Chandogya Upanishad 5.4–9). The soul is carried to heaven by the cremation fire whereupon the gods offer it "into the fire that is the heavenly world" and it becomes the sacrificial liquid called soma. The soma is then offered into the rain cloud, "and from that offering springs rain." Rain falls to earth and becomes food, and food is "offered" (i.e., eaten) by the "fire," which is man and is transformed into semen. The semen is emitted into the woman, and a new fetus takes form. This sacrificial circulation of souls is thus portrayed as a series of transmutations of various substances: the soul becomes soma, soma becomes rain, rain becomes food, food becomes semen, and semen produces the new body the soul takes on in the next life.

Other texts resort to metaphors to describe rebirth. Reincarnation is compared to the changing of clothes as the soul sheds one body for another: "As a man discards worn-out clothes to put on new and different ones, so the embodied self discards its worn-out bodies to take on other new ones" (Bhagavad Gita 2.22). In the following, rebirth is portrayed as similar to a caterpillar moving from one blade of grass to another, or a weaver who weaves a "newer and more attractive" design out of her yarn:

It is like this. As a caterpillar, when it comes to the tip of a blade of grass, reaches out to a new foothold and draws itself onto it, so does the self, after it has knocked down this body and rendered it unconscious, reaches out to a new foothold and draws itself onto it. It is like this. As a weaver, after she has removed the coloured yarn, weaves a different design that is newer and more attractive, so the self, after it has knocked down this body and rendered it unconscious, makes for himself a different figure that is newer and more attractive—the figure of a forefather, or of a Gandharva (celestial being), or of a god, or of Prajapati, or of *brahman,* or else the figure of some other being.

—Brhadaranyaka Upanishad 4.4.3–4

The possibilities for the kind of rebirth one can receive are virtually unlimited. In addition to birth as an ancestor, god, or other celestial figure (or as a demon or resident in hell), Hindu texts claim that one can be reborn into a new human life (of various sorts and conditions) or as an animal or even a plant. "Some enter a womb by which an embodied self obtains a body. Others pass into a stationary thing—according to what they have done, according to what they have learned" (Katha Upanishad 5.7). Birth as a "stationary thing" is obviously not very desirable, for, among other reasons, it is not easy to move on from such a birth. According to one text, when souls have been recycled through various natural phenomena and fall again to earth in the form of rain, they take on the next existence as plants. The plant-soul must then wait until a man eats it in order to be transformed into semen and subsequently a new human being: "On earth they spring up as rice and barley, plants and trees, sesame and beans, from which it is extremely difficult to get out. When someone eats that food and deposits the semen, from him one comes into being again" (Chandogya Upanishad 5.10.6). Or, again, the soul-bearing rain is said in the following to result in rebirths of various types (depending, one assumes, on which kind of animal eats the plant that arises from the rain)—although the text is careful to note that everything is guided by karma, by "his actions and his knowledge": "After they have become rain, it rains them down here on earth, where they are born again in these various conditions—as a worm, an insect, a fish, a bird, a lion, a boar, a rhinoceros, a tiger, a man, or some other creature—each in accordance with his actions and his knowledge" (Kausitaki Upanishad 1.2).

Rebirth as a despised animal can also be held out as a punishment for those whom the authors of Hindu texts find reproachable. A woman who is unfaithful to her husband is not only "an object of reproach in this world; (then) she is reborn in the womb of a jackal and is tormented by the diseases born of her evil."[16] Traditional Hinduism also accounts for the variety of and differentiation between human beings in such terms. The theory of karma coupled with the doctrine of transmigration and rebirth can be employed to explain physical or mental deformities and deficiencies: "Thus, because of the particular effects of their past actions, men who are despised by good people are born idiotic, mute, blind, deaf, and deformed" (Manu Smrti 11.53). This same text goes into great detail by way of explaining the various types of physical consequences in the next life for wrongdoers of different sorts: a man who steals grain will be born missing a limb, a thief of food will suffer from indigestion, a horse thief will be lame, and so forth.

The doctrine's principal social ramification, however, is to legitimate and underpin the caste system in traditional Hindu India. Social inequality was rationalized in large part by recourse to karma and rebirth. Inequalities in the present life are the natural and just result of past karma, and the inequalities of a projected future will reflect the rewards and punishments of action in the present: "Now people here whose behaviour is pleasant can expect to enter a pleasant womb, like that of a woman of the Brahmin (the priestly class), the Ksatriya (the warrior class), of the Vaisya (agriculturalist and trader) class. But people of foul behaviour can expect to enter a foul womb, like that of a dog, a pig, or an outcaste woman" (Chandogya Upanishad 5.10.7). Note the equation here between rebirth as a dog or pig—both extremely impure and despised animals—and that as an outcaste.

Rebirth can also function to give hope to those who make efforts to be virtuous but slip along the way. Reincarnation can thus provide those who try and fail (i.e., most of the human race) with a second chance. The god Krishna tells Arjuna just such a thing; no attempt at virtue—even if it fails to reach perfection, even if one becomes "fallen in discipline"—is ultimately for naught but will bring about good results in the future:

> Arjuna, he does not suffer doom in this world or the next; any man who acts with honor cannot go the wrong way, my friend. Fallen in discipline, he reaches worlds made by his virtue, wherein he dwells for endless years, until he is reborn in a house of upright and noble men. Or he is born in a family of disciplined men; the kind of birth in the world that is very hard to win. There he regains a depth of understanding from his former life and strives further to perfection, Arjuna.
>
> —Bhagavad Gita 6.40–43

For most Hindus, in the present and in the past, the goal of life is to live virtuously and obtain, as a result, a better rebirth. But a few also strive to obtain the highest religious end posited by the Hindu tradition, freedom or liberation from rebirth. Sometimes this state is described as the attainment of "the world of *brahman*," an eternal state from which one is no longer reborn. Several texts distinguish a "path of the gods," which leads to this immortal state, from the "path of the ancestors," which entails rebirth. Those who have obtained true knowledge, who have re-linquished desire, and who no longer produce karma are promised such a condition after death:

> People like him pass into the flame (of the cremation fire), from the flame into the day, from the day into the fortnight of the wax-ing moon, from the fortnight of the waxing moon into the six months when the sun moves north, from these months into the year, from the year into the sun, from the sun into the moon, and from the moon into the lightning. Then a person who is not hu-man—he leads them to *brahman.* This is the path to the gods, the path to *brahman.* Those who proceed along this path do not re-turn to this human condition.
>
> —Chandogya Upanishad 4.15.5

Such an afterlife entails a kind of mystical union with the Cos-mic One, the unifying principle of the cosmos. For "a man who does not desire," that is, one who does not produce karma that fuels rebirth, the death of the body is followed by the eternal im-mortality of the liberated soul: "Now, a man who does not de-sire—who is without desires, who is freed from desires, whose desires are fulfilled, whose only desire is his self—his vital func-tions do not depart. *Brahman* he is, and to *brahman* he goes" (Brhadaranyaka Upanishad 4.4.6).

As we have seen, the Hindu tradition envisions many possi-ble afterlives and many possible rebirths, yet it is ultimately this final state of liberation, where one is free from both death and rebirth, that Hinduism holds up as the highest (and hardest) goal of human existence.

JUDAISM

Judaism, the religion, identifies as its authoritative source "the Torah," or "the teaching," defined as God's revelation to Moses at Sinai. Writings deemed canonical enter the category of Torah, though into that same category also fall all authentic teachings of every age. The revelation myth of Judaism maintains that at Sinai God revealed the Torah in two media, written and oral. That is to say, while part of the revelation took written form, another part was formulated orally and transmitted through memorization. The tradition of Sinai may then come to concrete expression through any great sage's teaching. But the account of the position of Judaism set forth in these pages derives from the dual Torah, written and oral, as set forth in the Hebrew Scriptures and as interpreted by "our sages of blessed memory," the rabbis of the first seven centuries of the Common Era.

The Written Part of the Torah

We know the written part of the Torah as the Hebrew Scriptures of ancient Israel, or the "Old Testament." This is made up of the Pentateuch, or Five Books of Moses (Genesis, Exodus, Leviticus, Numbers, and Deuteronomy); the Former Prophets (Joshua, Judges, Samuel, and Kings); the Latter Prophets (Isaiah, Jeremiah, and Ezekiel); the Twelve Minor Prophets; and the Writings (Psalms, Proverbs, Job, Song of Songs (aka the Song of

Solomon), Ruth, Lamentations, Ecclesiastes, Esther, Daniel, Ezra, Nehemiah, and Chronicles). All translations from the written Torah come from the Revised Standard Version of the Bible.

The Oral Part of the Torah: The Mishnah, Tosefta, and Two Talmuds

Judaism identifies a philosophical law code called the Mishnah (c. 200 C.E.) as the first and most important of the finally transcribed components of the oral Torah. The Mishnah is a set of rules in six parts, made up of laws dealing with the hierarchical classification of holy Israel in these categories: (1) agricultural life; (2) the holy calendar, Sabbaths, and festivals; (3) women and family; (4) civil law and the administration of justice and the state; (5) the Temple and its offerings; (6) purity laws. A tractate, or compilation of teachings, called Abot, "the Fathers," attached to the Mishnah, commences, "Moses received Torah at Sinai and handed it on to Joshua, Joshua to elders, and elders to prophets. And prophets handed it on to the men of the great assembly," and onward down to the very authorities of the Mishnah itself. That is how the document is placed within the oral tradition of Sinai. In addition to the Mishnah, three other writings carry forward the legal tradition of Sinai: the Tosefta (c. 300 C.E.), a set of further legal traditions in the model of those in the Mishnah; the Talmud of the Land of Israel (c. 400 C.E.), a systematic amplification of thirty-nine of the Mishnah's sixty-two topical tractates; and the Talmud of Babylonia (c. 600 C.E.), a commentary to thirty-seven of the same. The two Talmuds treat in common the second, third, and fourth divisions of the Mishnah. The former takes up the first; the latter, the fifth; and neither addresses the sixth. In addition, tractate Abot receives its Talmud in a compilation, the Fathers according to Rabbi Nathan, of indeterminate date.

The Oral Part of the Torah: Midrash-Compilations

The work of commenting on the Mishnah and its legal traditions found its counterpart, among the same sages or rabbis, in the labor of commenting on books of the written Torah. This work produced Midrash, or exegesis, meaning the interpretation of Scripture in light of contemporary events by appeal to a particular paradigm, or pattern, that showed how Scripture imposed meaning on contemporary occasions. Those biblical books selected for intensive amplification are the ones read in the synagogue: Genesis, in Genesis Rabbah (c. 400 C.E.); Exodus, in Mekhilta Attributed to Rabbi Ishmael (of indeterminate date but possibly c. 350 C.E.); Leviticus, in Sifra (c. 350 C.E.), and also in Leviticus Rabbah (c. 450 C.E.); Numbers, in Sifré to Numbers; and Deuteronomy, in Sifré to Deuteronomy (both c. 350 C.E.). In addition, Midrash-Compilations serve four of the scrolls read in synagogue worship: Lamentations, read on the 9th of Ab to commemorate the destruction of the Temple; Esther, read on Purim; Song of Songs, read on Passover; and Ruth, read on Pentecost. The Mishnah, Tosefta, Talmuds, and Midrash-Compilations together form the authoritative canon of Judaism in its formative age, the first seven centuries of the Common Era. All translations of portions of the oral Torah in this book come from those made by the author.

CHRISTIANITY

The Christian faith understands itself to be grounded in the Holy Spirit, God's self-communication. Access to the Holy Spirit is possible because in Jesus Christ God became human. The Incarnation (God becoming flesh, *caro* in Latin) is what provides the possibility of the Divine Spirit becoming accessible to the human spirit.

Speaking from the perspective of Christian faith, then, there is a single source of theology: the Holy Spirit, which comes from the Father and Son. But the inspiration of the Holy Spirit has been discovered and articulated by means of distinct kinds of literature in the history of the church. By becoming aware of the diversity of those sources, we can appreciate both the variety and the coherence of Christianity.

The Scriptures of Israel have always been valued within the church, both in Hebrew and in the Greek translation used in the Mediterranean world. (The Greek rendering is called the Septuagint, after the seventy translators who were said to have produced it.) Those were the only scriptures of the church in its primitive phase, when the New Testament was being composed. In their meetings of prayer and worship, followers of Jesus saw the Scriptures of Israel "fulfilled" by their faith: their conviction was that the same Spirit of God that was active in the prophets was, through Christ, available to them.

The New Testament was produced in primitive communities of Christians to prepare people for baptism, to order worship, to resolve disputes, to encourage faith, and for like purposes. As a whole, it is a collective document of primitive Christianity. Its purpose is to call out and order true Israel in response to the triumphant news of Jesus' preaching, activity, death, and resurrection. The New Testament provides the means of accessing the Spirit spoken of in the Scriptures of Israel. Once the New Testament was formed, it was natural to refer to the Scriptures of Israel as the "Old Testament."

The Old Testament is classic for Christians because it represents the ways in which God's Spirit might be known. At the same time, the New Testament is normative: it sets out how we actually appropriate the Spirit of God, which is also the spirit of Christ. That is why the Bible as a whole is accorded a place of absolute privilege in the Christian tradition: it is the literary source from which we know both how the Spirit of God has been known and how we can appropriate it.

The term "Early Christianity" designates the time between

the second and the fourth centuries of the Common Era, the period during which the church founded its theology on the basis of the scriptures of the Old and New Testaments. Although Christians were under extreme—sometimes violent—pressure from the Roman Empire, Early Christianity was a time of unique creativity. From thinkers as different from one another as Bishop Irenaeus in France and Origen, the speculative teacher active first in Egypt and then in Palestine, a common Christian philosophy began to emerge. The period of Early Christianity might also be called a "catholic" phase, in the sense that it was characterized by a quest for a "general" or "universal" account of the faith, but that designation may lead to confusion with Roman Catholicism at a later stage, and is avoided here.

After the Roman Empire itself embraced Christianity in the fourth century, the church was in a position to articulate formally its understanding of the faith by means of common standards. During this period of Orthodox Christianity, correct norms of worship, baptism, creeds, biblical texts, and doctrines were established. From Augustine in the West to Gregory of Nyssa in the East, Christianity for the first and only time in its history approached being truly ecumenical.

The collapse of Rome under the barbarian invasions in the West broke the unity of the church. Although the East remained wedded to the forms of Orthodoxy (and accepts them to this day), the West developed its own structure of governance and its own theology, especially after Charlemagne was crowned as emperor of the Romans by Pope Leo III on Christmas Day in 800 C.E.

To severe arguments regarding political jurisdiction, East and West added doctrinal divisions. The pope was condemned in 876 by a synod in Constantinople for failing to stop a small change in the wording of the Nicene Creed, which has become accepted in the West. A papal legate in 1054 excommunicated the patriarch of Constantinople. Even that act pales in comparison with what happened in 1204: European Crusaders on their way to Jerusalem sacked and pillaged Constantinople itself.

European Christianity flourished during the Middle Ages, and Scholastic theology was a result of that success. The Scholastics were organized on the basis of educational centers, Thomas Aquinas at the University of Paris during the thirteenth century being the best example. During the periods of Early Christianity and Orthodoxy, theologies as well as forms of discipline and worship were developed for the first time. Scholastic theology was in the position of systematizing these developments for the usage of the West. At the same time, Scholastic theologians also rose to the challenge of explaining Christian faith in the terms of the new philosophical movements they came into contact with.

The Reformation, between the sixteenth and the eighteenth centuries, challenged the very idea of a single system of Christianity. Martin Luther imagined that each region might settle on its own form of religion. In England the settlement was on a national basis, while in John Calvin's Geneva the elders of the city made that determination. But in all its variety, the Reformation insisted that the Bible and worship should be put into the language of the people, and that their governance should be consistent with their faith.

From the eighteenth century until the present, Christianity in its modern form has been wrestling with the consequences of the rise of rationalism and science. The results have been diverse and surprising. They include Protestant Fundamentalism—a claim that the Bible articulates certain "fundamentals" which govern human existence—and the Roman Catholic idea of papal infallibility, the claim that the pope may speak the truth of the church without error. In both cases, the attempt is made to establish an axiom of reason that reason itself may not challenge. But modern Christianity also includes a vigorous acceptance of the primacy of individual judgment in the life of communities: examples include the Confessing Church in Germany, which opposed the Third Reich, and the current movement of Liberation Theology in Central and South America.

Today Christians may use many combinations of the sort of sources named here to articulate their beliefs, and the resulting pattern is likely to be as distinctive as what has been produced in the past.

ISLAM

The Qur'an

The single source that constitutes the basis of all inquiry into the religion of Islam is the Qur'an. Revealed to the Prophet Muhammad from 610 to 632 C.E., it is understood as God's own speech. That is to say, Muslims believe that the Qur'an is not merely inspired by God, it is exactly what God meant to say to the early Muslim community and to the world in general. Furthermore, God spoke to Muhammad (usually through the angel Gabriel) in Arabic, and to this day Muslims resist translation of the Qur'an into any other language. The Qur'an is about as long as the Christian New Testament. It is divided into 114 chapters (called *suras*), which range in size from a few verses to a few hundred. All but one of these suras begin with an invocation, "In the name of God, the Merciful, the Compassionate," and with these words pious Muslims begin all endeavors of importance. There are many translations of the Qur'an into English; that of A. J. Arberry (*The Koran Interpreted*, 1955) is widely recognized as the best and is used in this series, despite the unfortunate gender bias in Arberry's language.

The Qur'an describes itself as a continuation and perfection of a tradition of revelation that began with the Torah, revealed to the Jews, and the Gospels, revealed to the Christians. In fact, the Qur'an directly addresses Jews and Christians, urging them to put aside their differences and join Muslims in the worship of the one, true God: "Say: People of the Book! Come now to a word common between us and you, that we serve none but God" (The House of Imran, 3:56). Jesus and Moses are explicitly recognized as prophets, and the rules and pious regulations in the Qur'an fit in well with similar rules found in Judaism and Christianity. Of course, a special role is given to Muhammad, the seal of the prophets and the leader of the early Muslim community.

Sunna: The Prophet as Text

The Prophet Muhammad serves as the second "text" for Muslims. Unlike the Qur'an, which is the single source for God's divine word in Islam, the words and deeds of the Prophet are found in many different sources. When it comes to the Prophet, precise words are not as important as his general "way of doing things"; in Arabic, this is called the Prophet's *sunna.*

The Prophet Muhammad ibn ᶜAbd Allah was born almost six centuries after Jesus' birth, around 570 c.e., and for the first forty years of his life he organized trading caravans. Around the year 610, he began meditating in a cave near his hometown of Mecca. During these meditations he was overwhelmed by a vision of the angel Gabriel commanding him, "Recite!" This event changed his life forever and he began, slowly, to preach to his relatives and neighbors. After years of effort, Muhammad and a small group of followers moved to the town of Medina. This *Hijra,* the emigration of Muslims from Mecca to Medina in 622 c.e., marks the beginning of the Muslim calendar and was a turning point for the early community. In Medina, hundreds flocked to the new religion, and when the Prophet died in 632, he left behind thousands of believers. The survival of this early group is testified to by the almost one billion Muslims in the world today. Now, as then, Muslims see the Prophet as an example of the ideal believer. Muslims often name their boys after the Prophet, wear clothes like his, and try to live according to his precepts.

Hadith: Examples of the Prophet's Sunna

Muhammad's words and deeds were preserved and passed on from generation to generation in a form of oral transmission known as hadith. The Arabic word *hadith* means "story," and a typical hadith begins with a list of those from whom the story was received, going back in time to the Prophet. Following this list is the story itself, often an account of the Prophet's actions in a particular situation or the Prophet's advice on a certain problem. The list of transmitters is an integral part of the hadith; for example: "al-Qasim—ᶜA'isha—The Prophet said . . ." Here, al-Qasim (an early legal scholar) transmitted this hadith from ᶜA'isha (one of the Prophet's wives), who heard it directly from the Prophet. These stories were quite popular among early generations of Muslims, but no one attempted to collect and organize them until over a hundred years after the Prophet's death. Two important early collections of hadith are those by al-Bukhari (d. 870) and Muslim ibn al-Hajjaj (d. 875). Hadith are also found in works of history and in commentaries on the Qur'an. It is worth emphasizing that Muslims do not believe that Muhammad was divine. A careful distinction was maintained between divine words, which originated with God and therefore were put into the Qur'an, and Muhammad's general advice to his community. Both sets of words were spoken by the Prophet, but the first were written down and carefully preserved, while the second were handed down through the more informal vehicle of hadith.

Tafsir: Commentary on the Texts

Today, as in previous ages, Muslims often turn directly to the Qur'an and hadith for guidance and inspiration, but just as often, they turn to commentaries and interpretations of these primary sources. These commentaries, or *tafsir,* concern themselves with questions of grammar, context, and the legal and mystical implications of the text. They expand the original source, often collecting interpretations of many previous generations together. The results can be massive. The Qur'an, for instance, is only one volume, but a typical commentary can be twenty volumes or more. The importance of commentary in the Islamic tradition demonstrates that the Qur'an and sunna of the Prophet are not the only sources for guidance in Islam. Rather, Muslims have depended on learned men and women to interpret the divine sources and add their own teachings to this tradition. Therefore, these commentaries are valuable sources for understanding the religious beliefs of Muslims throughout the ages. Together with the Qur'an and hadith, they provide a continuous expression of Islamic religious writing from scholars, mystics, and theologians from over fourteen centuries.

BUDDHISM

Upon examining the major bodies of sacred literature in Buddhism, it must first be noted that Buddhism does not define "canon" in the same sense that the Judaic, Christian, and Islamic religions do. First of all, scriptures comprising a Buddhist canon are not deemed authoritative on the basis of being regarded as an exclusive revelation granted to humans by a supreme divine being. In principle, the ultimate significance of a given scriptural text for Buddhists lies less in the source from whom it comes, or in the literal meanings of its words, than in its ability to generate an awakening to the true nature of reality. Texts are principally valued according to their ability to enable one to engage in practices leading to an enlightened state of salvific insight, which liberates one from suffering, although they can also be utilized to serve other vitally important if less ultimate purposes, such as the cultivation of compassionate ethics, explication of philosophical issues, and protection from obstacles to personal well-being. Buddhism is also distinctive in that it has never established any one body that has functioned in an equivalent manner to the Rabbinate, Episcopate, or Caliphate, charged with the determination of a single, fixed, closed list of authoritative works for the entire tradition. On a local level, Buddhist canons, based on the hermeneutical standard of privileging the realization of enlightenment over source and word, have tended to remain open (to varying degrees) to the inclusion of new scriptures over the course of history.

It should not be concluded that the factors discussed above have ever substantially limited the amount of sacred literature produced in Buddhism or have relegated scripture to a status less than primary in the religion's history. On the contrary, the various major Buddhist collections of scripture are extraordinarily voluminous in size and have continuously occupied a most highly revered place in the tradition as primary sources of teaching.[1] Appeals to a scripture's provenance have indeed played a momentous role in Buddhist history, with a primary determinate of a text's canonicity being recognition of it as containing *buddha-vacana*, the "spoken word" of a Buddha, or enlightened being—usually Siddhartha Gautama or Shakyamuni Buddha (563–483 B.C.E.)—the Indian founder of the religion. To reiterate, one can be sure that the authority assigned to buddha-vacana is derived in part from its source, but what is of utmost import is its liberating power as an indicator of enlightened wisdom.

Insofar as we can determine it, the buddha-vacana, first transmitted shortly after the end of Shakyamuni Buddha's life by his main disciples, at first came to consist of two major sets of texts. The first set is known as Sutra, and it comprises the discourses of the Buddha (or in some cases of his disciples, but with his sanction), relating the events in his past and present lifetimes and his practical and philosophical teachings. The second set, known as the Vinaya, presents the ethical discipline and monastic rules that regulate the life of the *sangha*, or community, as they were laid down by the Buddha. Collectively, these two sets form the core of what is known as dharma, or Buddhist doctrine.

In addition, Buddhist canons include texts that provide further explanation and guidance in the Dharma, such as commentaries on the Sutras and Vinaya, treatises on philosophical topics, and ritual and meditative manuals. Broadly known as Shastra, or exegesis, this type of work derived its authority not from being buddha-vacana, but from being authored by those scholiasts, philosophers, and meditation masters who came to be regarded by later Buddhists as of the highest accomplishments and explicatory skills. Perhaps the most important genre of Shastra texts is the collections known as Abhidharma ("Further Dharma"), which consist of systematic analyses and classifications of doctrine composed by scholastic masters as early as three hundred years after the Buddha.

Despite general agreement among Buddhist traditions on the principle that the words of a Buddha and the further exegeses by great masters of philosophy and meditation are what constitute authority and canonicity, there has also been profound disagreement among these traditions about conceptions of what a Buddha is and what a Buddha teaches, and in turn about which masters best explicated the most efficacious and reliable means to liberation. In addition to such sectarian differences, various regional and linguistic divisions have contributed to the compilation of a number of separate canons. Thus, in speaking of the major sources of Buddhism that will inform these volumes, it is necessary to briefly identify the religion's major sectarian and regional divisions.

The Buddhist world today can be divided according to three major traditions, each of which traces its origins to developments in India, presently inhabits a more or less definable geographic region outside India, and subscribes to a distinctive body of scriptural sources, which the followers regard as the most authentic version of the Dharma. The Theravada ("Teaching of the Elders") tradition was the first of the three to historically form a distinct community (fourth century C.E.), and today it continues to thrive in the countries of Sri Lanka, Thailand, Myanmar (Burma), Laos, and Cambodia. The Theravada corpus of scripture—known as the Tripitaka ("Three Baskets") because of its division into the three sections of Sutra, Vinaya, and Abhidharma, described above—was rendered into written form in the Pali language by Sri Lankan elders in the first century B.C.E., but its origins are traced back to a council convened shortly after the end of the Buddha's life in the early fifth century B.C.E., during which his leading disciples orally recited the Buddha's words and began committing them to memory. Theravadins regard their texts as conserving the Dharma as it was originally taught and practiced by Shakyamuni and his most accomplished followers, who are known as *arhats,* or "worthy ones." Their Tripitaka establishes fundamental Buddhist teachings on the nature of suffering, the selflessness of persons, the impermanence of all phenomena, and the path of nonviolent ethics and meditation, which leads to liberating wisdom.

The second major Buddhist tradition—which has called itself the Mahayana ("Great Vehicle") because it has seen its teachings as superior to those of the Theravada and the other (now defunct) preceding early Indian schools—developed in the first centuries of the Common Era in North India and Central Asia, and has long since come to be the predominant form of Buddhism followed in the East Asian countries of China, Korea, Vietnam, and Japan. While the content of the Vinaya and Abhidharma portions of its canon is closely modeled (with notable exceptions) on texts from the earlier Indian schools (which Mahayanists have labeled collectively as Hinayana, or "Small Vehicle"), the Mahayana also presented a new, divergent scriptural dispensation in its Sutra literature. Composed originally in Sanskrit, these Mahayana Sutras were said to be a higher form of buddha-vacana, which had been kept from the inferior Hinayana Buddhists until the capabilities of humans had evolved enough to employ this more difficult, but also more efficacious, Dharma. Popular texts such as the *Perfection of Wisdom, Lotus, Teaching of Vimalakirti, Flower Garland, Descent into Lanka,* and *Pure Land* Sutras promoted a new spiritual ideal, the career of the paragon figure of compassion and insight, the *bodhisattva* ("enlightenment being"). Focusing on the philosophical and practical tenets espoused in these newly emergent Sutras, the great Indian masters of the first millennium of the Common Era composed explicatory treatises that would come to stand as centerpieces in the Mahayana canons. Most important are the works of the Madhyamika, or "Middle Way," school, which expounded on the central idea of *shunyata,* or "emptiness," and those of the Yogacara ("Yoga Practice") school, which developed influential theories on the mind and its construction of objective realities. The subsequent history of Mahayana as it was transformed in East Asia is a complex and varied one, but in the long run two practically oriented schools, namely the Pure Land and Meditation (commonly known in the West by its Japanese name, Zen) schools, emerged as the most popular and remain so today. These schools supplement their canons with texts containing the discourses and dialogues of their respective patriarchs.

The third Buddhist tradition to appear on the historical scene, beginning around the sixth century C.E., is the Vajrayana ("Thunderbolt Vehicle"), commonly known as Tantric Buddhism. The Vajrayana survives today in the greater Tibetan cultural areas of Asia, including the Himalayan kingdoms of Sikkim, Nepal, and Bhutan. Tantric Buddhists regard themselves as Mahayanists and include in their canon all of the major Mahayana texts mentioned above. However, the Vajrayana itself also claimed a new and divergent dispensation of the Buddha's word, in the form of texts called Tantras. While not philosophically innovative, the Tantras offered novel systems of meditative disciplines and ritual practices known as *sadhanas*. Followers of the Vajrayana maintain that the Tantras are the highest and final words of the Buddha, esoterically preserved until the circumstances were right for their exposure to humanity. As the name Vajrayana suggests, the uniqueness of the Tantras lies in their claim to be providing the most powerful and expeditious means of attaining enlightenment. Like their East Asian Mahayana counterparts, Tantric Buddhists also reserve a place of eminence in their canons for the compositions of their most accomplished masters, who are known as *mahasiddhas*, or "great adepts."

HINDUISM

What we in the twentieth century call Hinduism is in fact a set of religious practices that have developed over three thousand years of Indian history and have a great variety of textual sources. That history begins with the four Vedas—oral compositions of people who called themselves Aryans and who were the ancestors of many of the inhabitants of India today. The term *Veda* means "knowledge," and these four works make up the accompaniment to Vedic sacrifice—the main form of worship for the early Aryans. Sacrifice usually involved an animal or vegetable offering to one of the many Vedic gods. The first Veda, the Rig Veda, is the oldest (c. 1500 B.C.E.), and comprises the mythological hymns of the sacrifice. The second, the Yajur Veda, contains directions on how to conduct the ritual; the third, the Sama Veda, contains accompanying musical chants. The final Veda, the Atharva Veda, includes hymns for fertility, healing, and other everyday uses in the domestic context, apart from the public sacrifice.

The second set of works important to Hinduism is more philosophical in nature. These works are the Upanishads (c. 900–300 B.C.E.), and consist of speculation about the power behind the sacrifice, called *brahman,* and the nature of the sacrificing self, called *atman.* The Upanishads also contain the beginnings of a system of belief in reincarnation—more properly called the transmigration of the individual self—through the endless cycle of births, deaths, and sufferings, called *samsara.* The Upanishadic philosophers believed that the key to liberation from this cycle of suffering was the union between the atman and brahman. Around 200 B.C.E., these initial ideas were developed into an elaborate science of meditation called Yoga by the philosopher Patañjali. His treatise, the Yoga Sutras, inaugurated the system of yoga as we know and practice it today.

While the Vedas, Upanishads, and Yoga Sutras reflect the religious practices of the upper strata, or castes, of Indian society, there was very little textual evidence for popular religious practices until the emergence of the epics, the Mahabharata and the Ramayana. The Mahabharata is the story of the tragic war between cousins, the Kauravas and the Pandavas. The Ramayana depicts the exploits of Rama—a hero said to be the *avatar,* or manifestation, of the god Vishnu. In rescuing his wife Sita from the demon Ravana, Rama slays Ravana and rids the world of the evil. Many see these two epics as the source of popular theology prevalent in India today. They are the first texts that make extensive mention of the classical Hindu pantheon—Shiva, Vishnu, Brahma, and Devi, or the goddess. The Mahabharata is also the source of the Bhagavad Gita—the Song to the Lord Krishna, who, in human form, acts as a charioteer in the war. Particularly in the nineteenth and twentieth centuries, the Bhagavad Gita has inspired much popular devotion as a Hindu response to the Christian missionary movement.

Near the end of the period of the composition of the epics (c. 200 C.E.), many kings, especially in North India, began to patronize these popular deities and build temples to house them. Such temples had texts called Puranas attached to them; the term *purana* literally means "story of the olden times." Puranas are encyclopedic compilations that praised the exploits of particular deities—Vishnu, Shiva, Brahma, and Devi, mentioned above. Notoriously difficult to date, the Puranas range from 200 C.E. to 1700 C.E. Another important set of texts, called Dharma Shastras, emerged at about this period; these were elaborate law books that codified daily life according to rules concerned with purity and pollution. The most famous of these is the Manavadharmashastra, or the Laws of Manu. The Puranas and the Dharma Shastras provide the bulk of the material upon which the modern Hindu tradition draws, and they originate in all regions of India.

The wide geographical spread of the Puranas is partly due to the fact that devotional movements were not exclusive to the northern Gangetic plain, where the Vedas and Upanishads were composed, but were inspired equally by the South Indian, or Dravidian, civilizations. These devotional movements were called *bhakti,* literally meaning "belonging to." A bhakta is someone who "belongs to" a particular god and has chosen that god for devotion. Beginning in the eighth century C.E., the South Indian bhaktas wrote poetry that became an influential source for Hinduism. The collection of poems by the Tamil saint Nammalvar, the Tiruvaymoli, has attained the same canonical status as the Vedas and is called the Tamil Veda. In addition, the Bengali saint Caitanya inspired a bhakti movement devoted to Krishna in the late fifteenth century C.E.; his followers wrote treatises, among them the Haribhaktirasamrtasindhu and Haribhaktivilasa, that explain the theology and ritual of devotion to Krishna. Many northern and western Indian poets, such as Mirabai (b. c. 1420 C.E.) and Tukaram (1608–1649 C.E.), have contributed significantly to the huge corpus of bhakti poetry and theology that Hindus read and recite today.

The final major source for the study of Hinduism is the Vedanta philosophical tradition, whose development and systematization is attributed to the teacher Shankara in the ninth century C.E. Shankara, and his major successor, Ramanuja (twelfth century C.E.), developed their philosophy through commentaries, called *bhasyas*, on the two main texts of Vedanta—the Vedanta Sutras and the Brahma Sutras. These texts summarize the doctrine of the Upanishads, mentioned above. In his classic work, Brahmasutrabhashya, Shankara argues a philosophy of nonduality *(advaita)*. For him, the perceptions of the mind and the senses are simply *avidya*, ignorance. In ignorance we perceive a duality between subject and object, self and the source of self. This perception of duality prevents the self (atman) from complete identity with brahman. When complete identity is achieved, however, there is liberation of the self from all ignorance.

These manifold sources—the Vedas, the Upanishads, the epics, the Puranas, the Dharma Shastras, the diverse corpus of bhakti poetry, and Vedanta philosophy—make up the spiritual foundations of Hindu practice today.

NOTES

1. BUDDHISM

1. That is, the Pure Land established by the Buddha Amida (also called Amitabha) for the sake of those who put their trust in him to accomplish their salvation.
2. The phrase "Praise to Amitabha Buddha" (Namu Amida Butsu).
3. From *Popular Buddhism in Japan: Shin Buddhist Religion and Culture,* ed. Esben Andreasen (Honolulu: University of Hawaii Press, 1998), 132.
4. Ibid., 135.
5. *Samsara* is the cycle of birth and death that beings experience in multiple existences. See the section "Rebirth in the Six Realms, Rebirth in the Pure Land, and Nirvana" in this chapter.
6. *Samkharas* are the constituent dispositions, shaped by previous actions and experiences in this life but especially in those past, which, in turn, shape our experience of the world. A mind freed from the samkharas is able to see the world as it really is, without prejudice.
7. Dhammapada 153–54; *The Dhammapada,* trans. John Ross Carter and Mahinda Palihawadana (New York: Oxford University Press, 1987), 39.
8. Carter and Palihawadana, *The Dhammapada,* 220.
9. Andreasen, *Popular Buddhism in Japan,* 132.
10. Burton Watson, *The Lotus Sutra* (New York: Columbia University Press, 1993), 226.
11. Phra Prayudh Payutto, *Buddhadhamma* (Albany: State University of New York, 1995), 61.
12. See Ñanamoli, trans., *The Path of Purification* (Singapore: Singapore Buddhist Meditation Centre, n.d.), 247.

13. T. W. Rhys Davids, trans., *Dialogues of the Buddha* (Oxford: Pali Text Society, 1989), 2:23–24, translation modified.
14. Payutto, *Buddhadhamma,* 104.
15. See note 6 in this chapter.
16. Adapted from Steven Collins, *Selfless Persons* (Cambridge: Cambridge University Press, 1982), 107.
17. Ñanamoli, trans., *The Path of Purification,* 207.
18. E. W. Burlingame, trans., *Buddhist Legends* (Cambridge: Harvard University Press, 1921), 2:305.
19. Ibid., 2:306.
20. Ibid., 2:307.
21. Ibid., 2:305.
22. Soka Gakkai is a Buddhist tradition that traces its roots to Nichiren, a thirteenth-century Buddhist teacher in Japan.
23. Daisaku Ikeda, *Unlocking the Mysteries of Birth and Death* (London: Warner Books, 1988), 99.
24. Payutto, *Buddhadhamma,* 67.
25. Carter and Palihawadana, *The Dhammapada,* 110.
26. I. B. Horner, trans., *The Middle Length Sayings* (Oxford: Pali Text Society, 1990), 3:315.
27. Ibid., 3:316.
28. Ibid., 3:319.
29. Luis Gomez, trans., *The Land of Bliss* (Honolulu: University of Hawaii Press, 1996), 92.
30. See, for example, Donald Lopez, "A Prayer for Deliverance from Rebirth," in *Religions of Tibet in Practice* (Princeton: Princeton University Press, 1997), 442–45.
31. *Foundations of Mindfulness* from Nyanaponika, *The Heart of Buddhist Meditation* (New York: Samuel Weiser, 1975), 120.
32. Francis Varela, ed., *Sleeping, Dreaming, and Dying: An Exploration of Consciousness with the Dalai Lama* (Boston: Wisdom Books, 1997), 163–64.
33. Carl Becker, *Breaking the Circle: Death and the Afterlife in Buddhism* (Carbondale: Southern Illinois University Press, 1993), 99–100. The discussion here on the bardo is drawn from Becker.

34. Richard Gombrich, *Precept and Practice* (Delhi: Motilal Banarsidass, 1991), 270.

35. Ibid.

36. Quoted in Stephen Teiser, *The Scripture of the Ten Kings and the Making of Purgatory in Medieval Chinese Buddhism* (Honolulu: University of Hawaii Press, 1994), 27.

37. Quoted in Teiser, *Scripture of the Ten Kings,* 28.

38. David Germano, "Dying, Death, and Other Opportunities," in *Religions of Tibet in Practice,* 491.

39. John Strong, *The Experience of Buddhism* (Belmont, Calif.: Wadsworth, 1995), 28.

40. Ibid., 30–31.

41. Luis Gomez, trans., *The Land of Bliss,* 16

42. Andreasen, *Popular Buddhism in Japan,* 137.

43. Edward Conze, *Buddhist Scriptures* (New York: Penguin, 1959), 153–55, with some modifications.

2. JUDAISM

1. All translations in this chapter are Neusner's except where noted.

2. Two moments in the life of the sage formed the center of interest: origins, meaning the event of becoming a Torah-disciple, and the moment of death. Contrast the full-life account of Jesus in the Gospels.

3. Translation: Jules Harlow, in *Mahzor for Rosh Hashanah and Yom Kippur* (New York: Rabbinical Assembly, 1972), passim.

3. ISLAM

1. All quotations from the Qur'an are from the translation by A. J. Arberry, *The Koran Interpreted* (New York: Macmillan, 1955).

2. Ruhollah Khomeini, *Islam and Revolution,* trans. Hamid Algar (Berkeley: Mizan Press, 1981), 242.

3. Malik b. Anas, *al-Muwatta',* ed. Hasan ʿAbdallah Sharaf, 2 vols. (Cairo: Dar al-Rayan, 1988), 1:301.

4. Ibid., 1:298.

5. Khomeini, 354–55.

6. Naguib Mahfouz, *Sugar Street*, trans. William Hutchins (New York: Doubleday, 1992), 204–5.
7. Ibn Ishaq, *Sirat Rasul Allah*, translated by A. Guillaume as *The Life of Muhammad* (Karachi: Oxford University Press, 1978), 678.
8. Ibid., 682.
9. Hajji Chum of Zanzibar, *Utenzi wa nushuri*, translated in *Textual Sources for the Study of Islam*, ed. Andrew Rippin and Jan Knappert (Chicago: University of Chicago Press, 1986), 89.
10. Modified from A. J. Wensinck, *The Muslim Creed* (Cambridge: Cambridge University Press, 1932), 118–19. Wensinck takes this hadith from Muslim's famous collection.
11. Ibid., 163. The quotation is from al-Nasafi, *Bahr al-kalam.*
12. Ibid., 168.
13. Chum, *Utenzi wa nushuri*, 88.

4. CHRISTIANITY

1. See Bruce Chilton, *Pure Kingdom: Jesus' Vision of God*, Studying the Historical Jesus 1 (Grand Rapids, Mich.: Eerdmans, 1996).
2. See Bruce Chilton, *The Kingdom of God in the Teaching of Jesus* (London: SPCK; Philadelphia: Fortress, 1984). For discussion since that time, and particularly the contribution of Marcus Borg, see *Pure Kingdom.*
3. Acts 23:8 makes out that the Sadducees deny resurrection altogether, and that is also the judgment of Josephus. I have argued that, despite their unequivocal statements (or rather, precisely because they are so unequivocal), we should be cautious about what the Sadducees denied; see *The Temple of Jesus: His Sacrificial Program within a Cultural History of Sacrifice* (University Park: Pennsylvania State University Press, 1992), 82. The Sadducees' position is attributed to them only by unsympathetic observers, such as Josephus (*War* 2 § 165–66) and various Christians (Mark 12:18–27; Matt. 22:23–33; Luke 20:27–38; Acts 23:6–8).
4. For Jesus' characteristic attitude toward Scripture, see Bruce Chilton, *A Galilean Rabbi and His Bible: Jesus' Use of the Interpreted Scripture of His Time* (Wilmington: Glazier, 1984); also published with the subtitle *Jesus' Own Interpretation of Isaiah* (London: SPCK, 1984).

5. A common assertion is that Jesus accorded with accepted understandings of resurrection within Judaism; see Pheme Perkins, *Resurrection: New Testament Witness and Contemporary Reflection* (London: Chapman, 1984), 75. That is an unobjectionable finding, but it leads to an odd conclusion: "Nor can one presume that Jesus makes any significant contribution to or elaboration of these common modes of speaking." Perkins is not clear about what she means here or the basis of her assertion. Does warning the reader against presuming that Jesus had something original to say imply that he in fact said nothing original? Why speak of presumption at all, when there is an actual saying to hand? But the analysis of the saying is also confused because Perkins speaks of it as invented by Mark when it has anything new to say and as routine insofar as it may be attributed to Jesus. The discussion typifies the ill-defined program of trivializing the place of Jesus within the tradition of the New Testament by critics who once tended to exaggerate the literary aspirations of those who composed the documents.

6. That work, and Augustine's perspective in this regard, is discussed in *Evil and Suffering*, another volume in the Pilgrim Library of World Religions.

7. For a survey of attempts to explain this statement, see A. J. M. Wedderburn, *Baptism and Resurrection: Studies in Pauline Theology against Its Graeco-Roman Background*, Wissenschaftliche Untersuchungen zum Neuen Testament 44 (Tübingen: Mohr, 1987), 6–37. He comes to no finding regarding what view Paul meant to attribute to some Corinthians, but he seems correct in affirming that a simple denial on their part (despite the form of words Paul uses) is unlikely. More likely, Paul was dealing with people who did not agree with his teaching of a *bodily* resurrection.

8. For a discussion of the practice in relation to Judaic custom (cf. 2 Maccabees 12:40–45), see Ethelbert Stauffer, *New Testament Theology*, trans. J. Marsh (New York: Macmillan, 1955), 299 n. 544. In *A Commentary on the First Epistle to the Corinthians* (London: Black, 1968), C. K. Barrett also comes to the conclusion that the vicarious effect of baptism is at issue (362–64), although he is somewhat skeptical of Stauffer's analysis.

9. As Perkins puts it, "These associations make it clear that the resurrection of Jesus had been understood from an early time as the eschatological turning point of the ages and not merely as the reward for Jesus as a righteous individual" (*Resurrection*, 227).

10. The adjective does not mean "physical" as we use that word. Although that is a simple point, it apparently requires some emphasis. Scholars of Paul routinely assert that Paul is speaking of some sort of physical resurrection, when that is exactly what Paul denies. See Tom Wright, *What Did Paul Really Say?* (Grand Rapids: Eerdmans, 1997), 50.

11. At this point, Origen is reading First Thessalonians 4 through the lens of First Corinthians 15, just as later in the passage he incorporates the language of "mansions" from John 14:2.

12. See Stanley Romaine Hopper, "The Anti-Manichean Writings," in *A Companion to the Study of St. Augustine*, ed. R. W. Battenhouse (New York: Oxford University Press, 1969), 148–74.

13. See Jaroslav Pelikan, *The Christian Tradition: A History of the Development of Doctrine*, vol. 1, *The Emergence of the Catholic Tradition (100–600)* (Chicago: University of Chicago Press, 1971), 123–32.

5. HINDUISM

1. See my chapter on Hinduism in *Evil and Suffering*, another volume in this series. All translations in chapter 5 of *Death and the Afterlife* are Smith's except where noted.

2. Mahabharata 3, app. 1, no. 16, lines 70–126. Translated in *The Origins of Evil in Hindu Mythology*, by Wendy Doniger O'Flaherty (Berkeley and Los Angeles: University of California Press, 1976), 222–23.

3. Satapatha Brahmana 10.4.3.1–9. Translated in O'Flaherty, *Origins of Evil*, 218–19.

4. Linga Purana 1.70.300–342. Translated in O'Flaherty, *Origins of Evil*, 227.

5. Baudhayana Pitrmedha Sutras 3.2.3. Translated in *The Cultural Heritage of India*, vol. 2 (Calcutta: Ramakrishna Mission Institute of Culture, 1962), 411.

6. Bhagavad Gita 8.6–7. This and all subsequent references to this text are taken from *The Bhagavad-Gita: Krishna's Counsel in Time of War*, trans. Barbara Stoler Miller (New York: Bantam Books, 1986).

7. See my chapter on Hinduism in *Women and Families,* another volume in this series.

8. Markandeya Purana 10.47–87. Translated in *Textual Sources for the Study of Hinduism*, trans. and ed. Wendy Doniger (Manchester: Manchester University Press, 1988), 116.

9. This and all other quotations from the Upanishads are found in *Upanishads: A New Translation*, by Patrick Olivelle (New York and Oxford: Oxford University Press, 1996).

10. Visnudharmottara Purana (Bombay, no date) 116.1–12; 2.113–14. Translated in "Karma and Rebirth in the Vedas and Puranas," in *Karma and Rebirth in Classical Indian Traditions,* ed. Wendy Doniger O'Flaherty (Berkeley and Los Angeles: University of California Press, 1980), 16.

11. David M. Knipe, "*Sapindakarana:* The Hindu Rite of Entry into Heaven," in *Religious Encounters with Death: Insights from the History and Anthropology of Religions,* ed. Frank E. Reynolds and Earle H. Waugh (University Park: Pennsylvania State University Press, 1977), 111.

12. Markandeya Purana 10.47–87, translated in *Textual Sources,* 117.

13. The following is from Jaiminiya Brahmana 1.42–44, translated in *Tales of Sex and Violence: Folklore, Sacrifice and Danger in the Jaiminiya Brahmana,* by Wendy Doniger O'Flaherty (Chicago: University of Chicago Press, 1985), 32–35.

14. Brhadaranyaka Upanishad 4.4.5.

15. Vamana Purana 11.50–58; 12.1–42. Translated in *Classical Hindu Mythology: A Reader in the Sanskrit Puranas,* ed. and trans. Cornelia Dimmitt and J. A. B. van Buitenen (Philadelphia: Temple University Press, 1978), 50.

16. Manusmrti 5.164. This and subsequent quotations are from *The Laws of Manu,* trans. Wendy Doniger with Brian K. Smith (London: Penguin Books, 1991).

LITERARY SOURCES OF THE WORLD RELIGIONS

1. For example, a version of the Chinese Buddhist canon, published in Tokyo in the 1920s, is made up of 55 Western-style volumes totaling 2,148 texts!